Joseph McCabe

Twelve Years in a Monastery

Joseph McCabe

Twelve Years in a Monastery

ISBN/EAN: 9783743309043

Manufactured in Europe, USA, Canada, Australia, Japa

Cover: Foto ©ninafisch / pixelio.de

Manufactured and distributed by brebook publishing software (www.brebook.com)

Joseph McCabe

Twelve Years in a Monastery

CONTENTS

CHAPTER		PAGE
I.	Introduction	1
II.	Vocation	12
III.	Novitiate	30
IV.	Studentship	61
V.	Priesthood	90
VI.	The Confessional	113
VII.	A Year at Louvain	134
VIII.	Ministry in London	163
IX.	The London Clergy	186
X.	Country Ministry	214
XI.	Secession	233
XII.	Critique of Monasticism	251
XIII.	The Church of Rome	269

TWELVE YEARS IN A MONASTERY

CHAPTER I

INTRODUCTION

MONASTICISM, inseparable as it is from every great religious system, seems to emanate spontaneously from the fundamental religious idea. China, India, and Europe, despite their marked divergence in conceiving the ultimate objects of religious belief, and the distinct racial and territorial influences that have affected their development, have been equally prolific in monastic institutions—they seem to be evoked by the simple rudimentary story which is common to them all. And, indeed, we cannot wonder that that story has engendered an organised abdication of earthly joys such as the monastic system embodies. From the earliest ages, changing with their changes and ever growing with their measured roll, religion has taught men that the world about them was but a veil that hid a brighter world from their gaze, that, amidst the dreary ebb and flow of life, a spark of immortality dwells in the human breast, an inseverable bond with the unseen.

The story has been ratified by the acceptance of countless generations; it has crystallised into a thousand definite theological systems; it has inspired a wealth of sacred literature in every civilised nation. If then philosophers, from Crates to Fichte, on their cold reasonings, have been led to despise the changeful forms for the enduring realities their mind was thought to have glimpsed, it is not strange that the warmer, more vibrant tone of religion should have taught the same theme with yet deeper effect. For religion has gone far beyond the abstract results of philosophy, and has depicted to the imagination, with presumptuous but impressive vividness, the higher power and the larger life in which we are said to be enfolded. Men have gazed on the clear entrancing vision—its fair integrity and its unchanging joy mocking the precarious fulfilment of their soul's desire here below—until the attitude of hope and expectancy has satisfied them even now. In the hermit's cell or in the cloistered abbey they have withdrawn from earth and awaited, with the constancy of the hallucinated, the removal of the veil.

But the religious mind, at least in the western world, has entered upon a more troubled phase of its development. Physical and economical science have drawn its attention more eagerly to its present home:

a growing self-consciousness has made it more careful and introspective; the vision of hereafter has become blurred and indistinct. A large part—if not the larger part—of our latter day prophets, either abandon all hope of ever grasping the fading and intangible vision, or, at the most, pronounce it to be the unfaithful and distorted mirage of an inexplorable region. For the vast majority it has lost all the sharpness of outline and all the warmth of colour that once made it so potent an agency in human life. Compromise is the word. It *may* be true: and if the churches will temper their strictures so that they do less violence to present aims and ideals—well, like Pascal, men will remain on the safe side. But the age of martyrs, the age of Crusaders, the age of public penance, and even of private mortification, must hope for no revival. The sterner dictates of supernaturalism must be explained away as unsuited to a more sensitive and a more energetic age, or as a blunder in exegetics on the part of a less enlightened generation.

Hence, when, a few years ago, Dr. St. George Mivart, a writer of much eminence and erudition, confessed that he looked forward to a rejuvenescence of the religious orders of the thirteenth century, he was greeted with a smile of incredulity outside the narrow sphere of his own co-religionists. That Dr. Mivart, ardent evolutionist [1] as he is, should cling to

[1] Ardent, that is to say, from the Catholic point of view: his co-religionists have for years regarded his views as perilous, and

the old dispensation was surprising enough; though, indeed, it was suspected that he had his own mode of conceiving Catholicism, which, if the holy office had not put a prompt 'closure' upon him, might have been duly unfolded to the world. However, it seemed incredible that so broad-minded an interpreter of events should predict a revival of the great monastic orders; and (such is the irony of the relation between clergy and laity in the Roman Church), at that very time it was being whispered in ecclesiastical circles that Rome was thinking of suppressing most of the religious orders.

Outside the Church of Rome the thought, if it was noticed at all, was treated with quiet disregard, and attributed to a spasmodic attack of zeal on the part of its author. Monasticism was dying—not in the odour of sanctity. Men visited the venerable ruins of abbeys and monasteries, and re-peopled in spirit the deserted cells and dreary cloisters and the roofless chapel with a kindly archæological interest; smiled at their capacious refectories and wine-cellars; dwelt gratefully on the labours of the Benedictines through the Age of Iron; conjured up the picturesque life and fervent activity of the Grey Friars before their corruption, and shuddered at the zeal of the White Friars in Inquisition days. But people would as soon have

important manuals of theology stigmatise them in the strongest terms. He is, however, anti-Darwinian, and does not admit the evolution of the human mind.

thought to see the dead bones of the monks re-clothed with flesh as to see any great revival of their institutions. No doubt the system would die hard in countries that had resisted the angry Teutonic rebellion against Roman authority, but even in the warm lands of the South it was visibly decaying; never more would a Savonarola or a Jacobo della Marchia strike fire in the hearts of a multitude. Ecclesiasticism had become a profession, like the priesthood in later Judea or Greece or Rome, and it must be conducted on sober business lines at the risk of becoming distasteful.

In point of fact, however, there has been a revival of monastic institutions in our midst, proportionate to the revival of Roman Catholicism. A hundred years ago England flattered itself that the monastic spirit—if not Popery itself—was extinguished for ever within its ocean frontiers: the few survivors of the old orders were still proscribed and crept stealthily about the land in strange disguises. Then the French refugees surreptitiously re-introduced it—just as they brought over large quantities of the hated 'Popish baubles' in their huge boxes, which, on the king's secret instructions, passed the custom house untouched. The long Irish immigration set in, and the zeal of the aliens kept pace with growing British tolerance. The removal of Catholic disabilities, the Oxford movement, and the establishment of the hierarchy followed in quick succession, and, as Catholicism spread rapidly through the land, the Continental branches of the monastic orders grasped the opportunity of once more planting colonies on the fruitful British soil.

At the present day every order and congregation is represented amongst us, and the vast army of monks and nuns is many thousand strong. London, true to its encyclopædic character, embraces them all. Monasteries and convents are found in every large city in England, and often enough as one glides through our loveliest shires one sees from the train, nestling in the quiet valleys as in days of old, the severe quadrangular structure of some modern monastery. Any important ecclesiastical function in London attracts numbers of monks in their quaint mediæval costumes. After three long centuries they have started from their graves and are walking amongst us once more.

It is true that the fact is not much appreciated outside their own sphere, for the modern monks are not wholly unaffected by the world-evolution. The Benedictine does not bury himself with dusty tomes far from the madding crowd : he is found daily in the British Museum and nightly in comfortable hotels about Russell Square. The Grey Friar, erstwhile (and at home, even now) bareheaded and barefooted, flits about Suburbia in silk hat and patent leather boots and silver-headed cane. The irrepressible Jesuit is again found everywhere. Still, whatever be their inconsistency, they come amongst us with the same stereotyped profession, the same archaic customs and costumes of their long-buried brethren.

Their reappearance has provoked several controversies of actual interest. When the monks last vanished from the stage in England they left behind them a dishonourable record which their enemies were not slow to publish. Are modern monasteries and convents the same whitened sepulchres as their predecessors on whom the scourge of the Reformation fell so heavily? A strong suspicion is raised against them by their former history. The suspicion is confirmed by a number of 'escaped' monks and nuns who have traversed the land proclaiming that such is the case; although, it must be borne in mind, they usually come from that distant land which is not remarkable for the accuracy of its contributions to our literature. The impenetrable secrecy of monastic life is also far from reassuring.

On the other hand Roman Catholics appeal to their monastic institutions as an eloquent proof of their undying spiritual vitality. From the schismatic churches (such as the Anglican), the detached branches of the great tree of Christianity, the life has naturally departed; it flows on with perennial youth in the mother church of Rome. Rome alone can now inspire moral heroism, but Rome *can* do it, in spite of the rapid beat of time and the corroding forces of a sceptical age. She still holds up the loftiest Christian ideals to humanity, and her children embrace them in thousands.

And the monastic orders have been dragged also into the seething waters of the social problem. Now that Socialism has forced its way through the serried ranks of theologians and philosophers into the arena of honourable discussion, it has met with the usual solemn consecration from the Church, like Darwinism or the Higher Criticism. Christ is discovered to have been a Socialist : the early Church a model Socialistic community. And in proof that the Church did not abandon the Socialistic teaching of its founder under the shadow of imperial patronage and in the possession of regal power, monasticism is held up as an object lesson in Socialism that has never been absent from the Church. No doubt it is strange that the monks themselves, twenty or thirty years ago, anathematised Socialistic ideas as fervently as the rest of the faithful, but monks have never been the wisest section of the Church.

The most unpromising feature of the controversies that have thus arisen with regard to monasticism is that the disputants on both sides are deplorably ignorant of the true condition of monasteries. The Catholic layman, to whom the task of defending them is usually committed—it would be indelicate for the monks and nuns to defend themselves—usually knows as much of the interior and the *régime* of English monasteries as he does of those of Thibet. The monks preserve the most jealous secrecy about their inner lives: their constitutions strictly forbid them to talk of internal matters to outsiders, and their secular servants are enjoined a like secrecy with regard to the little that falls under their observation. Roman Catholics who live under the very shadow of monasteries for many years are usually found, in spite of a most ardent curiosity, to be completely ignorant of the ways of conventual life.

In such circumstances there is, perhaps, occasion for an ex-monk to contribute his personal experiences. The writer, after spending twelve years in various monasteries of the Franciscan Order, found himself compelled in the early part of last year to secede from the Roman Catholic priesthood. During those years, besides a long familiarity with the tenor of monastic life, a large experience of Catholic educational, polemical, and administrative methods has been accumulated, and it may not be inopportune to set it forth in simple narrative.

The religious order to which I had the good or evil fortune to belong is a revival of the once famous Province of Grey Friars, the English section of the Order of Saint Francis. At the beginning of the thirteenth century, immediately after the foundation of the Order, Agnellus of Pisa successfully introduced it into England. The English province (each national section of the order is called a province) flourished vigorously until the sixteenth century, and has put several distinguished names, such as those of Duns Scotus and Roger Bacon, on the rolls of English history. Of its later corruption and final overthrow at the Reformation it is unnecessary to treat; but, contrary to popular supposition, the Grey Friars (for they wore a grey habit in pre-Reformation days) were never really extinguished. From a monastery in France friars were sent over in various disguises, almost continuously up to the middle of the present century. About forty years ago the Belgian province of the same order, seeing that all hope of martyrdom in England was finally extinct, sent a colony for the purpose of reviving the order. Besides the rich spiritual emolument there were many attractions in the independent missionary life, and the Belgian friars offered themselves generously for the work. English novices were obtained, churches and monasteries erected, and ten years ago the English province found itself strong enough to form a detached organism. To-day it numbers eight large monasteries and more than a hundred religious in the United Kingdom.

Meanwhile, seeing the success of the brown-robed Belgian friars, the yellow-robed friars of the French province invaded the country from the south-west corner, and are also creeping apace. Each section claims to be the real successor of the original Grey Friars, and treats its rival as a usurper, whilst Rome, ever tactful and diplomatic, calmly encourages their rivalry for the ultimate growth of the Franciscan Order. A further complication arises from the fact that there is a third body claiming to be the original children of St. Francis—the bearded Franciscans or Capuchins.

Whatever may be the merits of their warmly-contested claims the Franciscan Order is largely represented by them in England. The Jesuit Society is still more numerous; the Benedictine, Dominican, Carmelite, and Carthusian Orders are also well represented, together with the minor congregations—Passionists, Marists, Redemptorists, Oblates, Servites, &c., and the infinite variety of orders and congregations of women. In the following pages I shall give such items of interest concerning them (and the Church of Rome at large) as may have fallen under my experience. As the narrative follows, for the sake of convenience, the course of the writer's own life, it is necessary to commence with the means of recruiting the religious orders and the clergy in general.

CHAPTER II

VOCATION

In pre-Rationalistic days a description of the means of recruiting the monastic orders (and the clergy generally) would have been simplicity itself. The vocation to that higher state was invariably attributed to a special interposition of Providence; the individual soul heard a Divine call, and had but to obey and be thankful for the choice. But in later years a remarkable tendency has developed, even in the sanctuary, to respectfully exclude Providence from the arrangement of sublunary matters. One or two successful revolutions helped men to realise that royalty was not a divine institution; Providence was exonerated from the control of the political world. Now, the economic world and the hierarchy of society seem in danger of being handed over to the play of 'natural causes'; it is seriously doubted, even by many ecclesiastics, whether the distribution of wealth *is* an immutable divine arrangement after all. Even in sacred literature the divine influence is gradually fading from view; verbal inspiration is, of course, a hopeless fossil, and inspiration of any kind is growing alarmingly attenuated under the attentions of our modern Cheynes and Sayces. The God of Epicurus or of Victor Hugo is coming to the front in the vast modern Pantheon.

In individual actions also the psychological method of the modern historian, biographer, and novelist tends to reduce the operation of Divine grace to a minimum. St. Augustine, St. Francis, and St. Ignatius have been repeatedly exhumed from the religious catacomb and dissected, and their conversions have been reduced to the sphere of natural law. Auscultory hallucinations are now preferred to voices floating in the air, crying 'Tolle, Lege'; dreams are more congenial than visions, and exalted ideas in a neurotic or hysterical temperament are calmly substituted, even by spiritual writers, for 'voices speaking in the heart.' 'Vocations' to a spiritual life are usually admitted to be susceptible of a satisfactory 'human' explanation; the providential agency is wisely presumed to have merely presided over the more immediate and tangible agencies.

But in treating of modern vocations there are few cases in which even the psychological method will find matter of interest and romance. Monasteries and nunneries are no longer refuges of converted sinners, of disgusted *roués*, of maimed knights-errant, and betrayed women. One does not need the pen of a Huysman to describe the souls *en route* to the higher life of the religious world. The sources from which monasticism draws its adherents to-day are much less romantic, and much less creditable, it must be confessed.

Nine-tenths of the religious and clerical vocations of the present day are conceived at the early age of 14 or 15. As a general rule the boy is struck with the desire of the priesthood or the monastery precisely as he is struck with the longing for a military career. His young imagination is impressed with the dignity and the importance of the priest's position, his liturgical finery, his easy circumstances, his unusually wide circle of friends and admirers. The inconveniences of the office, very few of which he really knows, are no more formidable than the stern discipline and the balls and bayonets of the martial dreamer; the one great thorn of the priest's crown—celibacy—he is utterly incapable of appreciating. So he declares his wish to his parents—if the course has not, even, been already suggested to him—and they take every precaution to prevent the lapse of his inclination. In due time, before the contaminating breath of the world can sully the purity of his mind, he is introduced into the seminary or monastery, where every means is employed to foster and strengthen his inclination until he shall have bound himself for life by an irrevocable vow.

Such is the ordinary growth of a vocation to the clerical state. There are, of course, exceptions, but they are proportionately infrequent; very rarely does a man of maturer age now seek admission into the cloister. Occasionally a 'convert' to Rome loses his balance and, in the first rush of zeal, plunges headlong into ascetical excesses. Sometimes a man of more advanced years will enter a monastery in order to attain the priesthood more easily; monastic superiors are not unwilling, especially if a generous alms is given to a monastery, to press a timid aspirant through the episcopal examinations (which are less formidable to religious), and then allow him, with a dispensation from Rome, to pass into the ranks of the secular clergy. And there are cases, too, it must be added, when a man becomes seriously enamoured of the monastic ideal, and seeks admission into the cloister; rarely, however, does his zeal survive the first year of practical experience.

Apart from such exceptional cases, monasteries and seminaries receive their yearly reinforcements from boys of from 14 to 15 years. Nothing could be more distant from the Roman Catholic practice than the Anglican custom of choosing the Church at an age of deliberation, during or after the university career. The Catholic priesthood would be hopelessly impoverished if that, the only honourable course, were adopted. The earliest boyish wish is jealously consecrated, for Catholic parents are only too eager to contribute a member to the ranks of the clergy, and ecclesiastical authorities are only too deficient in agreeable applications for the dignity; the result is that, instead of a boy being afforded opportunities of learning what life really is before he makes a solemn sacrifice of its fairest gifts, he is sedulously preserved from contact with it through fear of endangering his vocation. Too often, indeed, he is unduly influenced by the eagerness of his relatives, enters a seminary or convent for their gratification, and, if he has not the courage to return, to the disappointment and mortification of his friends, he bears for the rest of his life a shattered or depraved heart under his vestments of silk and gold. For it must be remembered that before he reaches what is usually considered to be the age of deliberation he is chained for life to his oar in the great galley—the bark of Peter—as will appear in the next chapter.

In the case of the present writer, there was happily not the faintest trace of undue family influence. Anxious as my parents were to see me in the ranks of the clergy, they were too humane even to manifest their eagerness, and they earnestly impressed upon me their desire for my return in case the new life should not suit me. Since, however, my vocation was of the normal kind, and may serve as a typical instance of monastic recruiting, it may be useful to describe it briefly.

My boyhood and early youth were spent under the shadow of the beautiful Franciscan church at Manchester. In spite, however, of the deep impression made upon me by the lovely Gothic edifice, and its imposing services, and the keen pleasure which I took in assisting in the sanctuary, I have a distinct recollection that up to the age of thirteen my mind was deliberately closed against the idea of entering the monastery. The friars frequently suggested the thought in playful mood, but I invariably repulsed their advances. At length a lay-brother[1] with whom I spent long hours in the sacristy exerted himself to inspire me with a desire to enter their Order. After many conversations I yielded to his influence, and conceived a desire for admission. In the meantime a violent quarrel had removed my family from the congregation, and seemed to have raised an insuperable obstacle on both sides. However, still haunting the neighbourhood, I was one day approached on the subject by the prefect of studies, confessed my willingness, and was subsequently admitted to preliminary studies.

Then, owing to the opposition of the superior of the monastery, I was cast adrift once more, and devoted myself, with little concern, to a preparation for the Civil Service. My name, however, was not forgotten at the monastery (to which the preparatory college was attached), and a new prefect of studies

[1] The inmates of a monastery are divided into two sharply distinct categories, clerics (priests and clerical students) and lay-brothers. The latter are usually men of little or no education, who discharge the menial offices of the community. They are called lay-brothers in contradistinction to the students or cleric-brothers, who, however, familiarly go by their Latin name 'Fratres.'

renewed the effort for my admission. I complied, after some hesitation, with an invitation to the monastery, and eventually it was arranged that I should be received as a pupil and aspirant to the monastic life. I had been conscious throughout of merely yielding to circumstances, to the advice and exhortation of my elders; there was no definite craving for the life on my part, certainly no 'voice speaking within me' to which I felt it a duty to submit. I do not, of course, mean to say that my subsequent profession was in any way a matter of constraint—once within the walls of the monastery my mind was seriously and deliberately formed (with whatever seriousness a boy of sixteen is capable of); I am merely describing the manner in which a religious 'vocation' is engendered. About the same time a Jesuit, the late F. Anderdon, S.J., made advances to me from another direction; and a third proposal was made to send me to the diocesan seminary to study for the secular clergy. There seem to have been no premonitory symptoms in my youthful conduct of the *enfant terrible* I was destined one day to become.

The 'vocations' of most of my fellow-students, and of my students in later years, were of a similar origin. They had either lived in the vicinity of a Franciscan convent or their parish had been visited by Franciscan missionaries. Already troubled with a vague desire for a sacerdotal career, the picturesque brown robe, the eventful life, and the commanding influence of the missionary—often, too, his suggestive words—had completed their vision. They felt a 'vocation' to the Order of St. Francis: their parents, if they were at all unwilling, were too superstitious to resist; the missionary was communicated with (after an unsuccessful struggle on the part of the parish priest to get the boy for the diocesan seminary), and the boy of thirteen or fourteen was admitted to the monastic college.

Other religious orders are recruited as a rule in a similar fashion. The more important bodies, Jesuits, Benedictines, and Dominicans, have more reliable sources of supply in their large public schools at Stonyhurst, Douai, and Downside: in such institutions the thoughts of the more promising pupils can easily be directed into the higher channels of religious aspiration by the zealous monks, without any undue influence whatever. But the ordinary congregations in England are sorely pressed for recruits—in fact, many of them were glad to accept the small fish that were cast back even from the net of the Franciscans. I have often heard their superiors lamenting England's barrenness (Ireland furnishes most of the recruits). 'It is all tea and coffee in this blessed city,' I heard a Superior of the Servites lamenting, 'we can get no religious vocations.'

Missionaries are the principal recruiting-sergeants. In fact the duty of the missionary is much more complex than appears at first sight. Besides holding the 'revival' services for the good of souls, he has several important functions to discharge for his monastery—the procuring of funds and the attraction of neophytes. Five pounds per week, besides a large amount of alms for masses to be said, is the lowest price a friar will accept for his pious services: and in proportion to his success in inspiring vocations will be his superior's thoughtfulness in appointing him to the more comfortable missions. For the modern missionary is not so insensible to the charms of hospitality as his mediæval forerunner.

The ranks of the secular clergy are recruited by similar methods. Large numbers of boys, usually of the middle and poorer classes, are drafted annually into the preparatory seminaries to be preserved jealously in their vocation if they have one, or inspired with one if they have not. Parents and parish priests are continually on the watch for symptoms of the Divine call, and in the case of clever quiet boys the wish is not infrequently father to the thought.

Finally, a word must be here said of the vocation of nuns: more will be said of them in the following chapter. It is true that the proportion of women who take the veil in maturer years is much larger than that of men; whatever may be their ultimate attitude it must be admitted that there is a large amount of earnestness and religious sincerity in the vocations of women. Still the number of young girls who are received into nunneries is lamentably high, and the anxiety shown by nun-teachers to inspire their pupils with a 'vocation' is extremely deplorable. They frequently request priests to secure aspirants for their congregations, and many a priest is tempted, out of desire to find favour at the convent (an important social distinction), to welcome the first word that his girl-penitents breathe in the confessional about a religious vocation. Many priests develop a perfect mania for sending their penitents to convents. For myself, in my hours of deepest faith I never found courage to send a girl to a nunnery: one girl, a penitent of mine, often solicited me about her vocation: I am thankful to say that I restrained her.

A conspicuous advantage of this system (from the ecclesiastical point of view), is that it affords time for a more extensive and systematic training. If other Christian sects—though they do not even impose an obligation of celibacy on their clergy—prefer the more honourable course of not extending any ecclesiastical sanction whatever to aspirants until they arrive at a deliberative age, they must and do suffer in consequence in the training of their ministry. The divinity lectures which the Anglicans follow are but a feeble substitute for the specialised education which their grave responsibility as religious teachers obviously demands; and in a large proportion of cases the theological training of Anglican curates begins and ends with such lectures. In later years, when contact with earnest readers impresses them with a due sense of their position, they are not infrequently heard to desiderate the systematic training of their Romanist rival. No doubt in point of general culture they are much superior to the average priest: one can often recognise the priest who has entered the sanctuary in a maturer age after secession from Anglicanism by that impalpable 'culture' which is the characteristic gift of our English Universities.

How it happens *in praxi* that the Catholic educational system produces such equivocal results will appear subsequently; in theory it is admirably constructed for the attainment of the ecclesiastical aim. Instead of merely adding a few lectures on current theological squabbles or patristic research to an ordinary liberal education, it takes the boy of thirteen or fourteen and arranges his whole curriculum up to the age of twenty-four, with a direct relation to his sacerdotal ministry. The course of training thus extends over a period of ten or eleven years under direct ecclesiastical control. The boy is handed over by his parents and transferred to the seminary or to a preparatory college in connection with it, where his education is at once undertaken by clerics. All the larger dioceses have their own seminaries, though at the present moment a warm controversy exists as to the advisability of amalgamation or continued separation.

The scheme is divided broadly, according to universal ecclesiastical usage, into three sections.

The preliminary training consists of the usual course of classics and mathematics: the classics being more than usually expurgated (after an unsuccessful attempt, under Pius IX., to abolish them altogether), and the whole generously interlarded with spiritual and ascetical exercises. This stage extends over a period of five or six years on the average: at Ushaw it is continued up to the twentieth year, at Wonersh (the new seminary founded for the Southwark diocese by the able and estimable Father Byrne), it only occupies five years. To the 'humanities' succeeds a course of scholastic philosophy (of which more afterwards) which usually occupies two years, and which now usually includes a few carefully expurgated and commentated lessons on physical science—for ecclesiastics are beginning to take the bull by the horns (very gently, and with much soothing language). Finally the student is treated to a three years' course of theology, passes a severe examination, and is admitted to ordination. The various stages will be described more in detail as the writer passed through them.

Such is the scheme of education of the Catholic priesthood all the world over, with but few local variations. The mendicant orders and the minor congregations generally corrupt and mutilate it: the larger seminaries and the more important orders expand it. The Jesuits have the longest and fullest curriculum, and their educational scheme has the highest reputation. In reality the curriculum of the Jesuit student is protracted mainly because he has to spend long periods in teaching, during which his own studies are materially impeded. And if we are to judge their philosophy by its fruits one hardly sees any occasion for unusual admiration : to one who is widely acquainted with the Jesuits it is painfully obvious that it turns out only a large number of uninteresting mediocrities. Although the Jesuits have the finest Catholic schools in the country, and it need not be said that they have practically their choice of boys from them, it is not evident that, as a body, they show any marked superiority over their less-dreaded colleagues. They have not a single pulpit orator ; they have not one man eminent in science ; the present Stonyhurst astronomer, highly and deservedly respected as he is, would hardly lay claim to that title. They have no great name in literature. If the reputation of the Jesuits, which is floating vaguely in the air, were to be carefully analysed it might possibly be traced to a dozen Jesuit pens and a hundred Jesuit tongues.

The Dominicans and Benedictines also conduct their preliminary studies in a creditable manner in their well-known colleges, but most of the other religious bodies are extremely negligent in that stage of education. Each religious order is, of course, responsible for the education of its own neophytes. For the religious orders—the *regular* or monastic clergy as opposed to the *secular*—do not fall directly under the jurisdiction of the bishop of the diocese. Monks are irregular auxiliaries of the canonical army who are supposed to emerge occasionally from their mountain fastnesses to assist in the holy warfare. The monasteries of the same order in each land are grouped into a province, and the central authority, the provincial, exercises a quasi-episcopal jurisdiction over them. All the provinces are united under a common general at Rome, and there is a special Roman congregation to regulate the conflicts (not infrequent) of bishops and the monastic clergy. Hence monks have but few points of contact with episcopal authority, and indeed they are usually regarded with jealous suspicion by the bishop and the secular clergy. Cardinal Manning was known to cherish a profound antipathy to all religious orders except the Franciscan, and to the Franciscans he said with characteristic candour : ' I like you—*where you are* (in East London).' Indeed, nearly throughout England the monastic orders have been compelled to undertake parochial duties like the ordinary clergy.

However, the comparative independence of the monastic orders gives them an opportunity of modifying the scheme of education according to the pressure of circumstances, and the general result is extremely unsatisfactory. The low ideal of sacerdotal education which they usually cherish is largely explained by the strong foreign element pervading them. They have been founded, at no very remote date, by foreigners, and are still frequently reinforced from the Continent. And it will be at once conceded that the Continental priest (or even the Irish priest) does not attach a very grave importance to the necessity of culture. A priest has definite functions assigned him by the Church, and for their due fulfilment he needs a moderate acquaintance with liturgy, casuistry, and dogma: beyond, all is a matter of taste. Relying, in Catholic countries, upon the dogmatic idea and the natural reverence which his parishioners have for the priesthood, he does not concern himself with any ulterior means of conciliating and impressing them. The consequence is that a low standard of education is accepted, and those who have imported it into this country have been slow to realise the true condition of their new environment—to perceive that, in England at least, a clergyman must be a gentleman of culture and refinement. The effect is most clearly seen in a wanton neglect of classics. The Franciscan *régime*, at the time I made its acquaintance, may serve as a typical instance.

The preparatory college of the Grey Friars (for they retain the name in spite of the fact that they now wear the brown robe of their Belgian cousins) was, at that time, part of their large monastery at Manchester. Seraphic Colleges, as the Franciscan colleges are called (not with reference to the character of their inmates, but because St. Francis is currently named the 'Seraphic' Saint), are a recent innovation on their scheme of studies, on account of the falling-off of vocations amongst more advanced students. The college was not a grave incubus upon the time and resources of the friars at that period. One of their number, an estimable and energetic priest, whose only defect was his weakness in classics, was appointed to conduct the classical studies and generally supervise and instruct the few aspirants to the order who presented themselves. We numbered eight that year, and it may be safely doubted whether there was an idler and more mischievous set of collegiates in the United Kingdom. Our worthy professor knew little more of boys than he did of girls, and he had numerous ministerial engagements to fulfil in addition to his professorial duties. The rector of the college, a worthy and religious-minded but delightfully obtuse old Belgian friar, would have discharged his function equally well if he had lived on Mars.

In spite, however, of the discouraging circumstances we contrived to attain our object very rapidly. We were all anxious to begin our monastic career in robe and tonsure as soon as possible, and all that the order required as a preliminary condition was a moderate acquaintance with Latin—the language of the Liturgy. Our professor, indeed, had a higher but imperfectly grasped ideal: he added French and Greek to our programme. Physics and mathematics were unthought-of luxuries, and our English was left at its natural level—in most cases a rich and substantial Irish brogue; though at one time our professor inaugurated a course of Hebrew, learning the day's lesson himself on the previous evening. Still, taking advantage of the fact that I studied at my own home, and of the eccentric activity of my professor, I was enabled to present a list of conquests at the end of the year which at once secured my admission to the monastic garb. The list is a curious commentary on our *modus procedendi*: it comprised: (1) French Grammar and a modicum of French literature; (2) Greek Grammar, St. John's Gospel, one book of Xenophon, and a few pages of the Iliad!—which latter were crammed for the express purpose of disconcerting the examiner; (3) Latin Grammar, several lives from Nepos, two books of Cæsar, six orations of Cicero, the Catilina of Sallust, the Germania of Tacitus, the Ars Poetica of Horace, two books of Livy, two books of the Æneid, and fragments of Ovid, Terence, and Curtius. As I only remained at the college from June 1884 until May 1885 it will be recognised how much care and exertion were required in later years to correct the crudity of such a procedure.

Those were not the worst days of our Seraphic College. Our professor was an earnest and hardworking priest, though an indifferent scholar, an unskilful teacher, and burdened with many difficulties. But the time came when even less discretion was exercised, and not only were studies neglected but the youthful aspirants to the monastic life, living in a monastery, had more licence than they would have had in any college in England.

However, it is, perhaps, unprofitable to discuss an abnormal, rather than the normal, course of sacerdotal education. Ten years afterwards (two years ago) I was entrusted with the task of cleansing the Augean Stables, and the parting legacy I left to my colleagues was the solid foundation of a wiser and sounder system. But I pass on to my first acquaintance with the inner working of monastic life.

CHAPTER III

NOVITIATE

The novitiate is an episode in the training of the monastic, not of the secular, clergy: it is a period of probation imposed upon all aspirants to the monastic life. Religious of every order and congregation,[1] both men and women, must spend at least one year as 'novices' before they are permitted to bind themselves by the solemnity of the vows. During that period they experience the full severity and asceticism of the life to which they aspire, and they in turn are minutely observed and tested by their superiors. It is a wise provision: the least that can be done to palliate the gravity of taking such an irrevocable step. Since no formal study is permitted during its course, it necessitates an interruption of the 'humanities' of monastic clerics.

In the original intention of the founders of the monastic orders there was no distinction between clerics and lay members. Francis of Assisi, who was

---

[1] A *congregation* is a monastic institution of less importance and antiquity than an *order*.

not a priest himself, simply drew up a rule of life, a modified version of his own extraordinary life, and allowed his followers, after due probation, to bind themselves by vow to its fulfilment. In it he naïvely proscribes study: 'Let those who know not letters not seek to learn them.' However, although a plenary inspiration is claimed for him in his first composition of the rule, he soon recognised the necessity of a different treatment of his clerical brethren: Antony of Padua was appointed by him 'to teach theology to the brethren.' He had not been many years in his grave—his premature death was not unassisted by his grief at the growing corruption of his order (the saintly Antony of Padua had already been publicly flogged in the convent of Aracœli at Rome for his dogged resistance to the corruptors)—when the intellectual fever of the thirteenth century completely mastered the fraternity. Many friars still held to the policy of holy ignorance, and Roger Bacon was imprisoned in England and Duns Scotus was buried alive by his brethren at Cologne (according to their amiable rivals—the Dominicans): however, the friars were to be found in hundreds in all the great universities, even in the professorial chairs at Oxford, Paris, and Cologne. Gradually the lay-brothers became the mere servants of the priests; the studies of the clerics were duly organised.

At that time and until the present century the neophytes were men of a more advanced age. After twelve months of trial, prayer, and reflection they were permitted to make their vows or 'profession' from which there was no dispensation. In recent years, however, the practice of taking aspirants at an earlier age has developed so rapidly that one feels apprehensive of a revival of the old Benedictine custom of accepting children of tender years whose parents were determined that they *should* be monks, for financial or political reasons. Pius IX. effected an important change in this direction. 'Attenta raritate vocationum—seeing the fewness of vocations,' as he naïvely confessed (the confessions which Popes have made in their Latin encyclicals from time immemorial are not sufficiently appreciated), he decreed that there should be two sets of vows. It would be too serious an outrage on human nature to allow boys of sixteen to contract an utterly irrevocable[1] obligation of so grave a character; at the same time it was clearly imperative to secure boys at that age if the religious orders were not to die of inanition. So a compromise was effected: boys should be admitted to the monastic life at the age of fifteen for their novitiate, and should make what are called 'simple' vows at the age of sixteen. From the simple vows the Pope was prepared to grant a dispensation, and the General of the Order could annul them (on the part of the

[1] The pope claims *de jure* to have the power to dissolve solemn vows, but *de facto* they are practically insoluble. There is only one clear case on record where the power has been used: it need hardly be said that it was in favour of a member of a wealthy royal house.

order) if the neophyte turned out unsatisfactory. The 'solemn' or indispensable vows would be taken at nineteen, leaving three years as a kind of secondary novitiate.

Thus the criticism of the enemies of monasticism was thought to be averted, and at the same time boys were practically secured at an early age; for it will be readily imagined that few boys would care to make an application to Rome for a dispensation and return to disturb the peaceful content of their families—having, moreover, had twelve months' probation besides two or three years in a monastic college. It was a clever, a thoroughly Roman, *coup*. In justice to the monks I must add that I have never known a case in which difficulties have been put in the way of one who desired a dispensation: certainly the accusation of physical detention in monasteries or convents is without foundation. If the student was promising, their advice to him to reconsider his position would, no doubt, take a very urgent and solemn character; if he persisted, I feel sure they would conscientiously procure his dispensation. However, in my personal experience I have only known one instance; he had entered under the influence of relatives and endured the strain for two years, but wisely revolted at length, sought a dispensation, and took to the stage.

It is thus explained how the monastic career usually commences at such an early age. A visitor to the novitiate of any order (a privilege which is rarely granted) cannot fail to notice the extreme youth of most of those who are engaged in weighing the tremendous problem of an irrevocable choice. They have, as a rule, entered the preliminary college at the age of thirteen, and have been called upon to come to a decision, fraught with such momentous consequences, at the age of fifteen or sixteen.

The novitiate, as the convent is called in which the novices are incarcerated, is normally a distinct monastery: economy of space, however, frequently compels the monks merely to separate the wing of some existing monastery for that purpose. In either case the regulations for its complete isolation are very severe. The novices are never allowed to leave the monastery during that year for any pretext whatever, and they are permitted to receive but few visitors and to have little correspondence (which is carefully examined) with the outside world. The natural result is that their comparison of monastic and secular life is conspicuously onesided.

For the novitiate of the Franciscan Order a portion of their friary[1] at Killarney had been set aside. Though there is a distinct Irish branch of the order (which, with truly Celtic *bonhomie*, has adopted a more humane modification of the Franciscan rule) the English province has had a friary at Killarney for many years. The three enterprising Belgian friars

---

[1] It is well to note that a house of friars may be called with equal propriety a friary, monastery, or convent.

who invaded England forty or fifty years ago had the misfortune to pitch their tent at Sclerder in Cornwall. After a few years of barren struggle and discomfort they sailed over to the more hospitable sister isle and settled at Gorey in the County Wicklow, whence they were soon invited to the cathedral city of Killarney. Warmly welcomed by Bishop Moriarty and generously assisted by the people, they soon erected the plain but substantial building of rough limestone which catches the eye of the tourist on issuing from the station. The friary enjoyed an uninterrupted prosperity from its foundation, with the inevitable consequence that its inner life soon became much more remarkable for comfort than for asceticism. However, one or two small scandals, the advent of a hostile bishop, the impoverishment of the country, and frequent visits from authorities brought about a curtailment of the friars' little amenities. And when the place was finally chosen as convent of the novitiate the good friars put their house in order, tightened their girdles, and resigned themselves to a more or less regular discipline; for one of their most sacred principles is that novices must not be scandalized.

The first impression which the place produced upon me when I entered it at the end of May 1885 was one of profound melancholy and discontent. There was an extensive and well-cultivated garden attached, and before us was ever outstretched the lovely and changeful panorama of the mountains.

But the interior of the monastery with its chill, gloomy cloisters, its solemn and silent inmates, conveyed at once a deep impression of solitude and isolation. When we sat down to supper at the bare wooden tables on the evening of our arrival—my first community meal—widely separated from each other, eating in profound silence, and with a most depressing gravity, I felt that my monastic career would be a short one. A young friend had entered their novitiate the previous year and had ignominiously taken flight two days after his arrival: I found myself warmly sympathising with him.

However, since we were not to receive the monastic garb for a week or more, we were allowed a good deal of liberty, and my depression gradually wore off. It happened, too, that I was already acquainted with three of the friars, and soon became attached to the community. The first friar whom we had met, a laybrother, rather increased our trouble: he was already far advanced in religious mania and ascetical consumption, and did, in fact, die a year afterwards in the local asylum. The second we met, also a laybrother, did not help to remove the unfavourable impression.' His jovial and effusive disposition only accentuated his curious deformity of structure: his hands and bare toes diverged conspicuously from the central axis, one shoulder largely preponderated over its fellow, his nose was a pronounced specimen of the Socratic type, and a touch of rheumatism imparted a shuffling gait to the entire composition. Happily we found that the teratological department of the convent ended with these two.

Our novice-master or 'Instructor' at that time was an excellent and much esteemed friar of six-and-twenty years; we were soon convinced of his kindness, consideration, and religious sincerity, and accepted willingly the intimate relations with him in which our position placed us. The superior of the monastery likewise had no difficulty in securing our esteem. He was a kindly, generous, and upright man, but without a touch of asceticism. Tall and very stout, with dark twinkling eyes and full features, he was a real 'Friar of Orders Grey' of the good old times. He was a Belgian, but he had attained wide popularity in Kerry by acquiring a good Flemish parody of an Irish brogue, and constructing a genealogical tree in which some safely remote ancestor was shown to be Irish. His ideal of life was not heroic, but he acted up to it conscientiously; he was genuinely pious in church, fulminatory in pulpit and confessional, kind and familiar with the poor and sick, generous and a moderate disciplinarian in his convent.

A few lay-brothers and four other priests made up the rest of the community. There was a cultured and refined young friar, who, after a few years of perverse misunderstanding and petty persecution from his less sympathetic brethren, was happily rescued from his position by the hand of death. A second, a tall, eccentric friar, ultimately became a stumbling-block to his fraternity; another, a little, stout Lancashireman of earnest and spotless life and of a deeply humane and affectionate disposition, fell a victim, a year later, to typhus. Last, but not least, was a little rotund and rubicund Irishman of enthusiastic, unreasoning piety; kind, ascetical, hardworking, studious (for he studied everything, except religious evidences), he was a much respected figure in Irish missionary circles. The one rule he confided to young missionaries was said to be: 'Throw the fire of hell at them,' and with his own stentorian voice (though he told you he was consumptive, and that one lung had decayed already) he threw it with prodigious effect amongst the peasantry.

A few days afterwards we were duly clothed with the monastic garb. The 'clothing' has developed into an impressive religious ceremony, and, as there were six of us to be clothed on this occasion, and it was the inauguration of a new novitiate, the event was celebrated with much solemnity. The six tunics, 'habits' as they are called, of rough brown cloth with their knotted cords, were blessed and sprinkled with holy water in the sanctuary, and, after an eloquent sermon by the Dominican Prior from Tralee, we were enrobed with the consecrated garments, amidst much prayer and psalm singing and the audible groans of the impressionable peasantry.

Our heads had been shaven in advance, leaving a

bald uncomfortable patch on the vertex about the size of a cheeseplate, a symbol, it is said, of the crown of thorns of Christ's passion. The brown tunic is also symbolical of the passion, for it is made in the form of a cross, the body being of the same width from neck to foot, and the wide sleeves branching out at right angles. However, the symbolism is an outgrowth of more modern piety. Francis of Assisi made no fantastic choice of a costume; casting aside his rich garments at his conversion he merely adopted the costume of the Italian beggar of his time—a rough tunic and hood, girded with a knotted cord, and sandals to his feet. The habit which excites so much comment on the modern friar is thus merely an Italian beggar's costume of the thirteenth century; substantially, at least, for it has fallen under the iron law of evolution. In fact the point of vital importance on which the two great branches of the Franciscan Order diverge is the sartorial question, what was the original form of the habit of St. Francis? The Capuchins hold that his hood (or 'capuce') was long and pointed, and that he cultivated (or rather, neglected) a beard; their rivals—the Observantes, Recollecti, and Reformati—dissent, and their age-long and unfraternal strife on the subject became as fierce and alarming as the historical controversy of the Dominicans and Jesuits of the sixteenth century on the nature of grace. The Roman authorities had to intervene and stop the flow of literature and untheological language by declaring all further publications on the subject to be on the 'Index Expurgatorius' *ipso facto.*

The costume is still uncomfortable and insanitary: in summer the heavy robe and the rough woollen underclothing are intolerable; in winter the looseness and width of the tunic promotes an undesirable ventilation, and, with due respect to Edward Carpenter, sandalled feet are decidedly unhealthy. Their rule prescribes that the costume consist of 'two tunics, a hood, girdle, and drawers,' but the inner tunic is interpreted in England to be an ordinary woollen shirt; on the Continent it is a second tight-fitting tunic of the same brown material. A mantle of the same colour is usually worn out of doors, and is considered part of the costume during the winter.

The name of the novice is also changed when he enters the monastery, as a sign that he is henceforth dead to the world. The surname is entirely dropped, and the Christian name is changed into that of some saint of the Order who is adopted as patron; thus my own name was changed into Antony. We were now, therefore, fully fledged friars, and we entered at once upon the dull routine of the monastic life. The character of the life will be best understood by a detailed description of an ordinary monastic day.

At a quarter to five every morning one of the friars was awakened by his alarm clock, and proceeded at once to arouse the community. We novices, with the eye o our instructor constantly upon us, shot out of our rooms at lightning speed, but in most cases the process was not so simple. There were friars of all stages of somnolency: some, of extremely nervous temperament, heard the alarm themselves and perhaps rushed upstairs for a cold bath; the majority were aroused by a vigorous tap of the wooden hammer at their door accompanied by the pious salutation, 'Laudetur Jesus Christus,' to which they sleepily responded 'Amen' (so, at least, the sound was piously interpreted, though in point of fact the response had many variations from the half awakened friars, from 'Come in' to much more profane expressions); some slept so profoundly that the knocker-up had to enter their rooms and shake them violently every morning. When the round was completed (all the bedrooms opening into a wide central corridor) the large bell sent a deafening clangour through the dormitories, and we quickly prepared for chapel.

A quarter of an hour was allowed for the purpose, but, as our toilet was simplicity itself, most of the friars who had got beyond the stage of primitive innocence continued their slumbers for five or ten minutes. We were directed by the constitutions to retain all our underclothing during the night, so nothing remained but to throw on the rough brown robe and gird it with the knotted cord; then towel in hand we raced to our common lavatory, for our simple cells of twelve feet square were not encumbered with washstands and toilet tables. In the lavatory a long narrow zinc trough with a few metal basins and a row of taps overhead was provided for our ablutions; I afterwards discovered that, crude as it was, this arrangement was rather luxurious for a friary.

At the end of the quarter the bell rang out its second warning, and all were supposed to be kneeling in their stalls in the choir by that time. The superior's eye wandered over the room to see if all were present, and any unfortunate delinquent was at once sent for, and would have to do public penance for his fault at dinner. At five the religious exercises began and continued, with half an hour's interval, until eight o'clock.

The ancient monastic custom of rising at midnight for the purpose of chanting the 'Office' finds little favour with modern monks; and even from a religious point of view they are wise. I was enabled to make observations on the custom some years later on the Continent, and I found little to be enthusiastic over, as Roman Catholic writers (usually those who have never tried it) frequently are. A few neurotic devotees enter into the service with their usual fervour, but the vast majority, to whom a religious concentration of thought during an hour's service is an impossibility even in their most lucid hours, are fatally oppressed with sleep and weariness. In summer they fall asleep in their stalls; in winter the night's repose is lost, and many constitutions are ruined by the hour or hour and a half spent in the icy-cold chapel at midnight. From no point of view is there occasion for sympathy and admiration.

The Office which is thus chanted in choir is a collection of Latin psalms, hymns, and lessons from Scripture which every priest is bound to recite every day. The monks chant it, or rather 'psalmody' it, in a monotone in their chapel at various hours of the day: the principal section, 'Matins and Lauds,' are the opening ceremony in the morning. It lasts about an hour, and is followed by a half-hour of silent meditation—broken only by the slumbers of the somnolent and the elderly brethren. A facetious London priest, who once endeavoured to pass through the novitiate of a monastery, maintains that he was discharged because he snored so loudly during meditation as to disturb the slumbers of the elderly brethren. Mass followed, and then breakfast was taken in profound silence. It was a simple meal, consisting only of coffee (taken in bowls and without sugar—except on fast-days) and bread and butter: during its progress a few pages of the 'Imitation of Christ' were read aloud. After breakfast a further section of the Office was chanted, and we were dismissed to arrange our rooms: for every friar, even the highest superior, is his own chamber-maid.

Afterwards we were allowed a quarter of an hour in the garden in strict silence, and then our semi-religious studies and classes commenced. During the novitiate profane study is prohibited (the perusal of a Greek grammar one day brought me as severe a reprimand as if it had been a French novel) and the time is occupied with religious exercises, of which we had seven or eight hours daily, and the study of our rule and constitutions, of ritual, and of ascetical literature. At half-past eleven another section of the Office was chanted, at twelve there was a second half-hour of silent contemplation (an injudicious custom — St. Teresa rightly maintained that one cannot meditate fasting), and at 12.30 the welcome dinner bell was heard. Growling, rather than reciting, a 'De Profundis' for departed benefactors, we walked in silent procession to the refectory, where, standing face to face in two long rows down the room, we chanted a long and curiously intonated grace.

Dinner was dispatched in strict silence : two friars read aloud, in Latin and English alternately, from Scripture or some ascetical work, and the superior gave the necessary signals with a small bell that hung before him. There were no table-cloths (for monks are forbidden the use of linen) but our pine tables were as smooth as marble and scrupulously clean. The friars only sit on one side of the table, on benches fixed into the wall, so that the long narrow tables run round the sides of the room. The windows were frosted, for we were overlooked by the police-barracks, whose English and Orange inmates were provokingly interested in our proceedings. The dinner itself was frugal but substantial enough: it usually consisted of soup, two courses of meat and two vegetables, and fruit—with a pint of beer to each friar. Many of us had hardly reached the age of strong drinks, but we were obliged to take our two pints daily (at dinner and supper) with the rest, and frequently a few glasses of wine in addition.

After dinner tongues are loosened at last, and recreation is indulged in until 2.30. There is a curious custom for two of the friars (a priest and a student) to wash the dishes after dinner. A large tank of hot water containing the dishes is suitably mounted in the kitchen, and the two friars, armed with cloths tied to the end of sticks, hurry through their task, chanting meanwhile alternate verses of the 'Miserere' in Latin, freely interspersed with ejaculatory comments on the temperature of the water.

The recreation is, in all monasteries, a very desultory episode, and usually resolves itself into a walk round the garden, chatting or disputing together. We were allowed cricket at the commencement of our term, but it was quickly vetoed by a foreign authority as contrary to religious modesty. Tennis and handball are also indulged in by the students. The lay-brothers play dominoes and the priests often follow their example, but the three sections—priests, students, and lay-brothers—may never intermingle; they are never even permitted to speak to each other without necessity. Cards are expressly forbidden; bagatelle is popular; and I have known the priests of a London monastery to occupy their recreation with *marbles* for many months. It was quite startling to hear such problems as Predestination or Neo-Malthusianism discussed over a game of marbles.

At 2.30 the bell summons them to choir for Vespers, the last section of the Office, and shortly afterwards tea is announced by the same medium. Nothing is eaten, but each friar receives a large bowl of tea; many of the older friars take another pint of beer instead, for tea is a comparatively recent innovation. The Belgian friars and the early English missionaries always take beer. Silence is not enforced during the quarter of an hour which is allowed for tea, but at its termination the strictest silence is supposed to be observed until recreation on the following day. In point of fact, however, the law of monastic silence is only observed with any degree of fidelity by novices and students, and by these only so long as the superior is within earshot. 'Charity,' they would plead in justification, 'is the greatest of all commandments.' Still, such as it is, the practice engenders a marked neglect of the commonest forms of politeness.

After an hour of prayer and spiritual reading we continued our pious studies until 6.30, when a third half-hour of silent contemplation had to be accomplished. It was pitiful, sometimes, to see young students endeavouring to keep their attention screwed upon the abstract doctrines of Christianity for so long a time—to see them nervously tightening their lips against the assaults of the evil one. For our monastic literature, never entertaining for a moment the idea that such a performance was beyond the powers of the average normally-constituted individual, taught us to see in spirit myriads of ugly little demons (why the devil should always choose or make an *ugly* body to appear in is problematical—the modern conception of him, *à la* Marie Corelli, is much more plausible) with pointed ears and forked tails, sitting on our shoulders and on the arms of our stalls and filling our minds with irrelevant thoughts. In fact, our worthy novice-master (and several respectable authors) assured us that the imps had been seen on more than one occasion by particularly pious elder brethren—that on one dreadful occasion, happily long ago, a full-sized demon had entered the choir with a basket and orthodox trident, discovered a young friar who was distracted in his prayers, and promptly disappeared with him in his basket. All of which we were obliged to listen to with the utmost gravity and concern if we set any value upon our sojourn in the monastery.

So a series of mental apparatus, called methods of meditation, had been invented for the purpose of aiding the wayward human mind to fix its gaze on the things of the spirit without interruption. Unfortunately they were often so complicated as to make confusion worse confounded. The method which our instructor selected for us was quite an elaborate treatise in itself. I remember one of our novices confiding to me the trouble it occasioned him. The method was, of course, merely an abstract form of thought to be filled in with the subject one chose to meditate about. But my comrade, a clever ex-solicitor, had by some incomprehensible confusion actually mistaken it for the subject of meditation, and complained that the bell usually rang before he had got through the scheme, and that he had no time left to tackle the particular virtue or vice he had wished to meditate upon. On the whole, it will be readily understood that of the seven hours of prayer which were imposed upon us at that period six at least were a pure waste of time.

At seven we were summoned to supper—a simple meal of eggs or cold meat, potatoes and beer. Afterwards, on three evenings per week, we took the discipline or self-scourging. Each friar repaired to his cell for the purpose and flogged himself (at his own discretion) across the shoulders with a knotted cord, whilst the superior, kneeling in the middle of the corridor, recited the 'Miserere' aloud. Knowing that our instructor used to listen at our doors during the performance, we frequently gave him an exaggerated impression of our fervour by religiously flogging the desk or any other resonant surface. However, our instruments of torture were guaranteed to be perfectly harmless, even in the hands of a fanatic. I remember what mental threats we uttered against a bloodthirsty little Portuguese friar who told us tales (with the suggestion to imitate) of the way *they* took discipline; but before the end of the novitiate we had learned the true value of the edifying tales with which visitors invariably entertained the novices.

The remainder of the evening was spent in private devotions or spiritual reading, and at 9.30 we were obliged to retire. Our beds were quite in harmony with the rest of the establishment; straw mattresses with a few blankets were all that we received. Besides the bed a wooden chair and a plain desk with half-a-dozen necessary books completed the furniture of the cell; a small plaster crucifix was the only effort at mural decoration. Our dormitory was cut off from the others by a special partition which was locked every evening, for the regulations for our isolation were very stringent. Even the superior of the monastery was not allowed to enter our department except in the company of one of the older friars.

Such was the ordinary tenor of our lives throughout the year of the novitiate, and indeed it had few variations. Feast-days were the principal events we looked forward to, and it would be safe to assert that few boys would persevere in their condition if the feast-days were abolished. A score of festivals were indicated in the constitutions on which the superior was directed to allow conversation at dinner, and to give wine to the brethren: 'half a bottle to each' was the generous allowance of the constitutions. In ordinary monasteries, festivals are much more frequent, and conversation is indulged at dinner on the slightest pretext. In the novitiate, where a stricter discipline prevailed, we had usually two or three every month, and on the more important feasts the midday dinner assumed enormous proportions. At Christmas the quantity of fowl and other seasonable food which was sent in occupied our strenuous attention during a full week: in fact, all our convents had the custom of celebrating the entire octave of Christmas with full gastronomic honours. So many friends conceived the happy idea of sending a gift to the 'poor friars' that the larder became quite a magazine of Christmas fare.

The greatest event of the year, however, was the patronal feast of the superior of the monastery. He was a warm favourite in Killarney, and there were enough comestibles (and potables) sent in to store a ship, the two neighbouring nunneries, especially, and a host of friends, vying with each other in the profusion and excellence of gifts to honour his festival. Even when a feast-day coincided with a fast-day, the restriction in solids was usually compensated by a greater generosity in fluids; we young novices were more than exhilarated on one or two occasions when dinner had been opened with a strong claret soup, accompanied by the usual pint of beer and a glass of sherry, and followed by two or three glasses of excellent port—sometimes even champagne. The restriction to fish is not felt very acutely, either, in Killarney, where the lakes produce magnificent salmon, and where, by a most ingenious process of theological reasoning, *water-fowl are included under the title of fish.*

At the same time the monotony was equally disturbed by the occurrence of the fasts. Besides the ordinary fasts of the Church, the friars observe several which are peculiar to their rule, especially a long fast from the first of November until Christmas. However, there are few who really *fast*—that is, content themselves with one full meal per day—in this degenerate age, even in monasteries; abstinence from flesh-meat is the usual limit of their mortification. On the Continent, fasting, in the strict sense of the word, is much more frequently practised in monasteries, but an intensification of their usual idleness is the necessary consequence; in England, it is to the credit of the monks, and clergy generally, that they prefer industry to fasting, though it is hardly to their credit that they still make a profession of fasting. The Passionists are the only English congregation who cling to the practice with any fidelity, and their statistics of premature mortality are an eloquent commentary on the stupidity of the Italian authorities who are responsible for it.

And even the 'fasting' of modern times departs

not a little from the primitive model. I have seen the 'one full meal' which is allowed at midday protracted until four o'clock, and a partial meal has been introduced in the evening. Drink, of course, does not break the fast, except strong soup, chocolate, and a few other questionable fluids, a list of which is duly drawn up by casuists; any amount of beer or wine may be taken. And since it is, or may be, injurious to drink much without eating, a certain quantity of bread is allowed with the morning coffee; at night (or in the morning if preferred), eight or ten ounces of solid food are permitted. The Franciscans are much reproved by rival schools of theologians for their laxity in this regard, and the strained interpretation they put upon admitted principles. At one time a caricature was brought out in Rome depicting a Franciscan friar complacently attacking a huge flagon of ale and a generous allowance of bread and cheese in the middle of his fast. To the ale was attached the sound theological aphorism 'Potus non frangit jejunium—drink does not break the fast'; the huge chunk of bread was justified by the received principle 'Ne potus noceat—in order that the drink may do no harm,' and the cheese was added in virtue of the well-known saying, 'Parum pro nihilo reputatur—a little counts as nothing.'

Since there was no parish attached to the monastery at Killarney (which is the correct canonical status of a monastery), a few words must be said of the life of the priests. At that time it was a hopeless mystery to me, and it is principally from later observation and information that I am able to describe it. That it was far from a life of industry will be readily understood; occasional visits to the sick poor and the rendering of services to the secular clergy of the diocese constituted the whole of their external work. In our own church there was only one sermon per week, and there were six friars to share the work. Hence the greater portion of the day was at the personal disposal of the priest; and, as manual labour was considered beneath the dignity of the priest, and their irregular education had left them, with few exceptions, little or no taste for study, they were always eager for distractions to occupy their time. They were frequently to be met rowing or sailing on the lakes (always in their brown habits), or driving on side-cars through the loveliest parts of Kerry; and, in return, the parish priests whom they visited or assisted, paid frequent visits to the friary and helped them to fill up an idle hour with a cigar and a glass of whisky. A few years later, indeed, a large-minded superior transformed a conservatory in the centre of the garden into a cosy smoking-room, and his generosity was warmly and practically appreciated.

In point of fact, both whisky and tobacco were forbidden in our constitutions, but I have never yet seen a constitution in which a theologian could not find a loophole and pass through it with unruffled dignity. The tale of the old lady at Glasgow who lost her purse and prayed that it might not fall into the hands of a theologian is very shrewd. The conviviality of the priests, in our days, was confined to a small room at a safe distance from our wing of the house, but we frequently met one of the juniors moving stealthily along the corridor with the neck of a bottle peeping out from his mantle, and often, as we lay awake at midnight, we caught the faint echo from the distant room of 'Killarney' or 'The Dear Little Shamrock.'

The penances, too, were an interesting feature of the life, when observed in the case of one's companions. The common form of public penance is to kneel in the centre of the refectory during dinner, praying silently with arms outstretched until the superior gives permission to rise. The next in point of severity is to kneel without the hood, or with an inscription stating one's crime, or with the fragments of anything one has broken. For graver faults, especially of insubordination, a culprit is condemned to eat his dinner on the floor in the centre, the observed of all observers, for one or more days; and for an exaggerated offence his diet is restricted to bread and water. Confinement to the monastery for a long period, suspension from sacerdotal functions, and, ultimately, expulsion from the order, are the more grievous forms of punishment. Though monastic constitutions still direct that each monastery must have its 'prison' I do not think that formal incarceration is now practised in any part of the world. Apart, however, from these penances the whole scheme of discipline is crushing and degrading. For speaking a word in time of silence a novice would be forced to carry a stick in his mouth during recreation : he would be called upon at any time, for no fault whatever, to stand against the wall or in a corner of the room and make a fool of himself in the most idiotic fashion. Everything is done to crush the last particle of self-respect, to distort and pervert character to monastic purposes.

I remember once nearly bringing my monastic life to a premature close by an act which any English schoolboy would feel bound in honour to do. A companion had playfully scattered a few blades of grass on me in the garden, and our instructor, inferring that I had been romping with him (a sin of the utmost gravity), asked me who was responsible for the presence of the grass on my habit. As the boy himself sat beside me on the bench I declined to speak, and the instructor departed without a word. Fortunately, or unfortunately, I was seized with a religious scruple immediately afterwards, and hastened to apologise. I found the instructor holding a grave *tête-à-tête* with the superior on the matter, and had I not apologised in a public and humiliating manner for my 'fault,' I should have been forthwith expelled from the monastery. Certain characteristics of the Catholic clergy are only understood in the light of such an education.

Thus the twelve months passed smoothly by, and the time approached for us to take the 'simple vows.' The votes of the community are taken every three months on the merits of candidates for the order. The community is assembled for the purpose in the chapter room (a room in which the superior assembles his religious three times per week for prayer, exhortation, and public confession of their minor faults—breaking utensils, oversleeping, &c.) and the superior invites a discussion on the merits or demerits of the novice. He then produces a bag of white and black marbles, of which he gives a pair to each voter: they are collected with great secrecy in two bags, and if the novice does not obtain a majority of 'white balls' he is significantly invited to abandon his intention. If it is probable that he will be 'blackballed,' he is usually warned in advance: hence it very rarely happens.

Our votes having been satisfactorily obtained we prepared to make our religious profession at the completion of our year of probation. The profession, an impressive religious ceremony, consists essentially of a vow to observe the rule of St. Francis and to 'live in poverty, chastity,' and obedience for the whole time

---

[1] A vow of chastity embraces the obligation of celibacy and much more: it doubles the guilt of any transgression of the virtue of chastity or purity, which, in the theory of the Church of Rome, is a

of our lives.' When the morning arrived a large and sympathetic congregation had gathered in the little church, and the sight of the six young friars—mere boys we all were—solemnly casting off every earthly hope with all the energy of aged Stoics, moved them deeply. The purport of the vow was explained to them in the exhortation of our superior, and they at least keenly felt the awful extent of our sacrifice. We, too, were convinced that we fully realised the gravity of our step: true, our thoughts were rather turned towards the glamour of the position we coveted and its many advantages, yet we were not insensible of the price we were asked to pay. But it was many a long year before the true gravity of the step could be realised, long after we had solemnly and irrevocably ratified our vows.

What are the world and the flesh to a boy of sixteen, or even to a boy of nineteen (at which age the final, irrevocable step is taken) who has been confined in an ecclesiastical institution from his thirteenth year? He knows little more of the life which he cuts off so lightly by his vow of poverty than he does of the life of Mars; and he is absolutely ignorant, when he makes his vow of celibacy, of that profound passion which will one day throb so powerfully in every fibre of his being and transform the world beyond conception.

very comprehensive piece of ethical legislation. Yet many confessors actually encourage their girl-penitents, living in the world, to make such a vow.

Yet he is permitted, nay invited, to make that blind sacrifice and place himself in life-long antagonism to the deepest forces of his being before he can have the faintest idea of his moral strength. If it be true that monastic life is ever sinking into corruption, we should feel more inclined to pity than to blame the monks.

The secular clergy make no vow of poverty or obedience, and it may be urged that even their vow of celibacy is more defensible. The seminary student makes his vow when he is admitted to the subdiaconate, the first of the holy orders, and the canonical and usual age of the subdeacon is twenty-one. The average youth of twenty-one may be admitted to be capable, in ordinary circumstances, of forming an opinion on such matters, but we must remember that the ecclesiastical student has had an abnormal training. Every precaution has been taken to keep him in blank ignorance of sexual matters, and to defer the development of that faculty of which he is asked to make a life-long sacrifice. He has never come in contact with the complementary sex, for even during his vacation the fear of scandal hangs like a mill-stone about him; he has never read a line concerning the most elementary facts and forces of life—his classics, his history, his very fiction have been rigidly expurgated; the weekly minute confession of his thoughts, the incessant supervision of his superiors, the constant presence of innumerable ethico-theological scarecrows, all have combined to postpone the unfolding of Nature's most wondrous gift until he shall have blindly abdicated it for ever. In the confessional I have known students of a much more advanced age who were still unconscious of its power. In fact the Church knows that they are unconscious, and expects them to be unconscious; for if she awaited the full development of mind and body in her candidates her clergy would never be sufficiently recruited.

The proportion of nuns who take the vow of chastity at an early age is smaller, as I have said but the sin is more grievous. The life of the nun who finds in later life that she has made a mistake is infinitely more wretched; the priest is in the world and frequently of it, the nun is jealously imprisoned in the walls of her convent. No doubt her vow is usually only a 'simple' vow and theoretically dispensable; but who ever knew a nun to write to Rome for a dispensation? No woman would dare to face the practical ignominy of such a step.

I have never been able to witness without a shudder the ceremony of a young girl making her vows. Some pachydermatous monk or veneered Jesuit preaches to her from the altar of the tranquil joy of her future life as spouse of Christ alone, and the candid virginal eyes that are bent upon him tell only too clearly of her profound ignorance of the sleeping fires within her, the latent joys of love and maternity which she sacrifices so readily. In ten years more she will know the meaning of the vow of chastity into which she has been deluded. It was brought home to me vividly on hearing, a few years ago, the confession of a young nun who was in the wild throes of passion-birth; after detailing the usual peccadilloes she began to tell me of her utter misery and isolation. Her sisters were unkind, thoughtless, and jealous; 'and yet, father,' she urged piteously, 'I *do* want someone to love me.' I muttered the usual commonplaces, but, as she knelt at my feet, looking sadly up at me, in their little convent chapel, I felt how dark a sin it was to admit an immature girl to a vow of chastity. How their parents—their mothers—can let them act thus without a word of warning surpasses my comprehension. 'Tis another signal instance, no doubt, of the triumph of grace over nature!

CHAPTER IV

STUDENTSHIP

AFTER the novitiate has been successfully accomplished it was necessary to resume the course of our education. Through the total neglect of profane study which is foolishly directed, most of the ground we had already conquered was lost during the year of the novitiate. Latin was sustained, even advanced a step, since all our services and quasi-religious studies had been in Latin—although ecclesiastical Latin, and especially the Latin of the psalms of which we heard so much, would make the shade of Cicero shudder. Whatever other acquisitions had been made were entirely lost. We had, therefore, to devote ourselves once more to 'humanities,' and for this purpose we were transferred (without a glimpse of the immortal lakes, for the friars had fallen on evil days with the bishop) to what is now the principal house of studies of the Franciscans at Forest Gate in East London.

The friars have to-day at Forest Gate a large and imposing pile of buildings, two schools, a fine but incomplete monastery, and a very spacious and handsome Gothic church. The foundation is an object of much pride to London Catholicism. Fifteen years ago there was no Catholic congregation in that locality. Then the friars from the Stratford monastery began to say Mass in a small outhouse of the Ursuline Convent to a dozen or so of Catholics ; a school-chapel was built, and the congregation had reached about 300 when our party arrived twelve years ago. Section by section the church, monastery and schools, representing about 20,000*l.* worth of property, were rapidly erected, and the congregation soon numbered more than 3,000. Rival churches were alarmed ; Roman Catholics dreamed extravagant dreams of the conversion of England.

But if one had made inquiries in neighbouring Catholic parishes the secret of the miraculous growth would quickly have been revealed. Nearly every priest in East London was exasperated against the friars for stealing his best parishioners. There were really few 'converts' to Rome in the new congregation, and those were merely the flotsam and jetsam of superficial religious controversy. The great bulk of the congregation were the better middle-class Catholics from all parts of East London who had migrated to the new and healthier district in which the friars had erected a church, mainly on borrowed funds.[1]

---

[1] It is curious to note that one of their principal benefactors has since seceded from the church. The secession was kept a profound

When we arrived at Forest Gate in 1886 the mission was in the hands of the three ablest friars of the order, F. David, F. Aidan, and F. Bede; the success of the mission was mainly due to the devoted exertions of the two latter friars, for F. David, a man of much erudition and ability, was intended rather for the supervision of our studies. He had been professor of philosophy at the friary in Ghent for ten years previously, and had, therefore, been chosen by the Belgian authorities to supervise the studies in the new English branch of the order. Unfortunately the long years of exclusive attention to study had made him extremely unpractical, and our studies proceeded in a most desultory and irregular fashion. There were so few of us in the community, and our professor had so many other offices to discharge, that little attempt was made during the first six months to organise our work. All our religious exercises were hurried through early in the morning, making more than three consecutive hours of prayer of divers kinds, and, as often as not, we had the monastery to ourselves during the day. Once or twice a week, at any hour of the day or night, our professor would interrupt the course of his ministerial and parochial duties and his studies of Sanscrit at the British Museum to

secret by the few of my colleagues who knew it, but was accidentally communicated to me.

'What has he become?' I inquired.

'Oh! a Theosophist or Agnostic, or something of that kind,' was the lucid reply of my discriminating colleague.

give us a class in Latin; even during that half hour he used to write letters, and we would purposely make the most atrocious blunders and conduct ourselves in the wildest manner our imagination could suggest.

Our long Saturnalia came to an end at last with the arrival of a second and younger professor, who entered into the work of reform with alarming zeal. He was fresh from the Belgian province, in which a perfect discipline (from a mechanical point of view) prevails in the houses of study. Young, intensely earnest, and sincerely religious, he made an honest effort to reform us without losing our sympathy, but, as he knew little more of our studies than we did, and had an uncontrollable temper, and a conspicuous harshness of character, he alienated us more and more as time went on. From Belgium too, he had imported the system of *espionage* which is deservedly odious to English students; he considered that the necessary rigour of monastic discipline justified it. However, he never cared to be caught in the act, and we gave him many a *maurais quart d'heure* by running to the door of our study room when we saw his shadow near it, and chasing him through the convent in his anxiety not to be seen. At length we appealed to authority, and effected his deposition and removal. In later years I learnt to esteem and respect him, and he made rapid progress in the order and in the

London ministry; finally, however, he ended in an ignominious apostasy and deep disgrace.

His successor proved to be a superior of quite an opposite character. Far from continuing the zeal and rigour of his predecessor, he became alarmingly broad and familiar, and before many months had elapsed we found it impossible to entertain a particle of respect for him. In point of fact he already showed clear symptoms of mental aberration, and a few years afterwards his conduct became (and still remains) so extraordinary that absolute dementia is the kindest hypothesis to urge in its defence. He, too, was removed from his position at our appeal, and we began to have an evil reputation in the province. During our five years of study at Forest Gate we succeeded in removing no less than six professors and superiors, and, since I was the 'dean' of the students all through my curriculum, I attracted an undue amount of interest; I have no doubt that my own 'fall' was frequently predicted many years in advance. Our immediate superiors came to bear the name of the 'Removables' in the province.

After twelve months at classics we were initiated into a course of rhetoric. The Jesuits more wisely postpone the rhetorical studies until the last year, but, in any case, it is little more than a waste of time. Lessons in elocution and declamation are decidedly opportune, and should be insisted upon much more

F

conscientiously than they are in the training of priests, but the usual 'course of rhetoric' is only learned to be forgotten. It deals with the invention and distribution of arguments, the analysis and composition of orations, the various styles of discourse, figures of speech, and the comparative play of ideas and emotions. There are few who retain any knowledge of its multitudinous rules when the period of practice arrives, fewer still who pay the slightest attention to them. The only useful element of the training is the practice of making ecclesiastical students prepare and deliver short sermons to their companions. In many monasteries the students preach to the assembled community during dinner. It affords excellent training for public speaking, for one who is able to speak with any degree of self-possession to a small audience will have little fear of a large congregation. I have often preached to a congregation of a thousand people with the utmost composure, but I have invariably trembled before a congregation of ten or twelve persons.

The course of rhetoric is succeeded by a course of scholastic philosophy. In the great mediæval schools philosophy was taught in conjunction with theology; to the arguments drawn from Scripture and tradition on any point of belief the professor usually added a few arguments 'from reason.' In the twelfth century there had been, of course, much philosophical activity; indeed, the main controversy of that fiercely argumentative age, the question of universals, was a purely philosophical problem. Still such questions merely arose incidentally from theological problems; in an age of unquestioning faith in the unseen, the formal and distinct treatment of philosophy as a preliminary science was unnecessary, the doctrinal points were merely confirmed 'from reason.' St. Thomas, however, led to a divorce by publishing, in addition to his 'Summa Theologica,' a smaller 'Summa Philosophica' or 'Contra Gentes' which purported to defend the more fundamental points of Christian belief without recourse to revelation; it was intended to appeal to the Arab or Neo-Peripatetic school, through which the schoolmen had become acquainted with Aristotle's philosophy. John Duns Scotus, the celebrated English friar, followed Aristotle's example more closely, and wrote many distinct treatises on logic and metaphysics. By the sixteenth century, when there was a conspicuous revival of speculative activity, the separation of philosophy from theology was complete. In our own logical and Rationalistic age such a separation is imperative. Before a positive revelation can be entertained certain preliminaries, notably the existence, nature, and authority of the Revealer, must necessarily be established by pure reasoning; hence philosophy must precede theology.

The scholastic philosophy which is taught in Catholic seminaries usually includes treatises on logic, metaphysics, and natural ethics. First is given a short treatise on dialectics, which differs little from the ordinary logic of Jevons or Whateley, and it is followed by a more careful study of the second or material part of logic. Just as the pressure of unbelief evolved the distinct science of philosophy, so the pressure of modern criticism, of Kantism and Empiricism, has lent a vast importance to material logic or 'Criteriology' as an introduction to scholastic metaphysics. The transcendentalist and the Empiricist, coming from opposite quarters, have joined forces in the destruction of pure metaphysics. The criteriology of the modern scholastic attempts to ward off their criticism by a vindication of the trustworthiness of our faculties and by the establishment of an available criterion of truth.

A treatise of general metaphysics follows in which are discussed, analysed, and vindicated the general concepts and principles which will be used subsequently in the construction of the desired theses; such are, causality, substance and accidents, time and eternity, finiteness and infinity, &c. Special metaphysics is divided into three parts, cosmology, psychology, and natural theology or theodicy. The division frequently changes, but the treatise is understood to discuss every object which comes within the purview of unaided human thought. It opens with a proof of the existence of the material world, against the Idealists, discusses its origin and its features of time and space;

then the question of life is entered upon, its origin and nature discussed, and the two great branches of the organic world are philosophically described and commented upon. The second part, psychology, is concerned with the human soul; it seeks to prove its spirituality and immortality against the Materialist, classifies and analyses its various faculties, treats of the origin and nature of thoughts, emotions, and volitions. The third part treats of God; it opens with the usual demonstration of His existence against the Agnostics, endeavours to elucidate His attributes as far as mere reasoning will avail (and the scholastic philosopher is persuaded that it will avail much), and considers His relations to this nether world.

The line of reasoning throughout is taken closely from Aristotle; the conclusions arrived at may be traced ultimately to certain general principles which are neither an accumulation of sense-impressions (against the Empiricists), nor merely subjective laws (against the Kantists)—they are intued directly by the mind, and are supposed to carry with them their own credentials of objective truth. Until the time of Thomas Aquinas, all Catholic philosophers (except Boetius) had followed Plato, and regarded Aristotle with suspicion; St. Thomas, however, and all the schoolmen, except St. Bonaventure, rejected the Platonist method and introduced Aristotle (through the Latin translations of the Arabic school), expurgated his philosophy, and enlarged it in certain directions in harmony with Christian teaching. Thus the scholastic philosophy is fundamentally the philosophy of Aristotle, who is always spoken of by the schoolmen as 'the philosopher,' just as St. Paul is called 'the Apostle.'

To logic and metaphysics is usually joined a treatise on natural ethics, founded on the Nicomachean ethics. It deals with the abstract conceptions of right and duty, virtue and vice, law and conscience; discusses the various theories of moral obligation; expounds and enforces the various duties which arise from the relations of individual, social, and international life. Since no appeal to revelation is admitted in it, the treatise goes by the name of natural ethics to distinguish it from the science of moral theology, which covers the same ground in the light of revelation and authority.

One of the principal defects of the course of philosophy which is thus given to clerical students is its narrow exclusivism. That their own philosophical system is plausible, strongly and cleverly constructed, is what one would expect from the vast number of keen intellects that have contributed to its elaboration; but every manual from which it is taught and every professor carefully excludes, or only gives a most inaccurate version of, rival philosophies. At Cambridge, the programme of philosophical authors is so delightfully impartial that few students find themselves in possession of definite philosophical views after reading it; in every seminary and monastic college the impression made upon the student is that the scholastic system is so clearly and uniquely true that all opponents are either feeble-minded or dishonest—usually the latter alternative is urged.

And, indeed, apart from the fact that all opponents (as writing 'expressly against faith') are on the Index, and that it would be a sacrilege to entertain the possibility of their being right for a moment, the time which is devoted to the vast subject is entirely inadequate. Two years is the usual duration of the course; one year is very frequently the limit of philosophical study. Then the ages of the students must be taken into account; they are generally youths of from eighteen to twenty-one who are quite incapable of entering into such grave problems seriously, and only one in a hundred makes any attempt to do so. Sufficient information is committed to memory to satisfy an examiner; but, unless the student is drawn to the science for a solution of questions that have arisen in his own soul (which is rarely the case), he shirks philosophy to the utmost of his power, and looks forward eagerly to his deliverance from it.

Its attractiveness is still further lost sight of on account of its injudicious treatment at the hands of professors; they are frequently men of little or no scientific attainments (though a wide acquaintance with science is essential to a philosopher), and, neglecting the problems of actual interest and importance, they fritter away the allotted time in the most contemptible controversies. The liberty of the will or the existence of God will be dismissed in a day, and a week will be zealously devoted to the question whether substance and personality are two distinct entities, or whether the qualities of a thing are physically, formally, or mentally distinct from its substance. In many seminaries a certain amount of physical science is taught in conjunction with the course of philosophy, but much jealousy is shown with regard to it. I was much attracted to the empirical sciences from the beginning, and, though not actually prevented, I was much discouraged in their pursuit; I was informed that the empirical sciences made the mind 'mechanical' and predisposed to materialism. F. David, though not actually my professor, guided my studies with great kindness throughout my course; although I fortunately broke loose from his influence in some directions, and found that I had subsequently to verify with care whatever I had accepted from him, I was certainly much indebted to him for the formation of habits of industry and precision.

The priest who was nominally entrusted with our philosophical training is certainly not responsible for the fatal depth to which I ultimately penetrated into it. One of the few things he had not mastered was metaphysics; he could paint and play, and was an authority in architecture, archæology, rubrics, casuistry, canon law and history. The authorities had the intention of making him our professor of theology, and it was thought that he could safely be entrusted with our philosophical studies in the meantime. He was a Belgian friar of noted eccentricity, and his method of teaching philosophy was quite original—a family of parrots could have passed his examinations as brilliantly as we did. After each lesson he dictated a number of questions and answers, and on the following morning the answers were to be repeated word for word. Some of my fellow-students passed a most satisfactory examination at the end of the term without having a single idea on philosophical questions. The worthy professor was another victim of our seditious movements.

The last three or four years of the student's career are devoted to the study of theology. Under that title are usually comprised ecclesiastical history, canon law, scripture, moral and dogmatic theology. Ecclesiastical history, usually a very narrow and one-sided version of the vicissitudes of the Church, does not, as a rule, occupy much of their time, and generally assumes an apologetical character. Canon law, a vast system of ecclesiastical legislation, is either entirely neglected or given in a very rudimentary fashion. Each order and diocese secures one or two experts in the subject, who are appealed to in case of complications, internal or external, but the majority of the clergy are content with the slight knowledge of canon law which they necessarily glean from their moral theology. The three years are, therefore, devoted to Scripture and theology proper.

With four lectures each week during a period of two or three years it is impossible to study satisfactorily more than a comparatively small section of the Scriptures. A general introduction precedes, dealing with the idea of inspiration, the formation of the orthodox canon of Scripture, and the history (usually in caricature) of Rationalism and the Higher Criticism; the special introduction to the New Testament endeavours to urge its claims to credibility as an historical narrative, by a host of internal and external arguments. Certain books are then selected for detailed commentary, and the students are supposed to study the exegetical method in order to cover the rest of the ground at their leisure.

How far is the study of Scripture in the Church of Rome affected by the Higher Criticism (and the monuments)? Very profoundly, in point of fact, though the modification of views can find no expression since the celebrated retrograde encyclical of Leo XIII., Newman's contention that there were *obiter dicta* in Scripture which did not fall under the inspiring influence introduced a far-reaching principle; it was not necessary to hold that *all* was inspired. Before the stern criticism of the Rationalists many had begun to admit scientific and historical errors in Scripture, even to contend for them in the pages of the 'Tablet'; and a celebrated French professor, M. Loisy, went very far in company with the critics. Then came the Pope's encyclical declaring that no errors could be admitted in Scripture, and M. Loisy disappeared from his chair (with a most suave and courteous letter from the Pope in his pocket, recognising his past services). However, an encyclical only affects the *expressions*, not the *thoughts*, of scholarly Catholics. Leo XIII. has never once used his 'infallible' authority; his encyclicals enjoy neither more nor less than his personal authority as a theologian—which, in serious quarters, is nil. He is an impressive *littérateur*, and his utterances are blindly accepted by the bulk of the faithful, not only as marvellously profound, but as sharing, to some extent, the prestige of his supernatural power; they are wrong on both counts. A Loisy or a Mivart will simply wait patiently until Cardinal Vanutelli or some broader-minded man assumes the tiara; at present, as a matter of discipline and policy, they must keep silent.

Another refuge from the oppression of the encyclical is in the elasticity of the word 'inspiration.' That the whole of Scripture is *inspired* is an article of faith; what *inspiration* is, has never been defined. The advanced thinker can give it any interpretation his views may demand. A very able professor of Scripture at Louvain University, assured me that his own ideas on Scripture were absolutely chaotical on account of the vagueness of the fundamental idea; he prayed for a dogmatic definition of inspiration.

Moral theology has been detached from dogmatic, in the specialisation of studies, and forms a distinct science of a purely practical nature. It opens with a few general treatises on moral responsibility, conscience, law, and sin, which constitute what is called fundamental theology. The special treatises which follow discuss the obligations of the moral agent in every conceivable relation and circumstance. Each treatise usually takes a particular virtue as its object, and enumerates every possible transgression of the same, arguing out their comparative gravity and frequently giving practical rules to the confessor in dealing with them. Thus there is a treatise on religion, which, after explaining the general obligations of the virtue, enters into a detailed discussion of its possible transgressions—sacrilege, blasphemy, &c.—giving numerous divisions and illustrations, and carefully drawing up a scale of their relative gravity. There is a treatise on impurity which gives the student the physiological elements of the subject and enumerates (with the crudest details) the interminable catalogue of its forms, the professor usually supplementing the treatise from his own experience in the confessional. There are, also, treatises on charity, on justice (a voluminous treatise which descends into the minutest details of conjugal, social, and commercial life), on veracity, and all other virtues.

Throughout the preceding section on virtues and vices, which usually forms a quarto volume of some 500 or 600 pages, little appeal is made to positive revelation. The pronouncements of the theologian are enforced from time to time by texts from Scripture and references to ecclesiastical legislation, but the main portion of the work is purely ethical and rational. The second section, however, treats of obligations which are wholly connected with their revealed dogmas: it discusses at great length (in a second quarto volume of 500 pages) the seven sacraments of the Church of Rome, the vast number of obligations they entail in practical life, the transgressions which arise from their neglect or abuse, the theory and the practice of their constitution. The two principal treatises are on confession and matrimony; in the former the future confessor receives the necessary directions for his task (a much more complicated one than is commonly supposed), and in the latter the numerous Catholic impediments to marriage and their dispensations are treated, and there is a further discussion of conjugal life. The path throughout is beset with the innumerable conflicts of theologians, and every point is profusely illustrated with real or fictitious 'cases.'

Moral theology is regarded as the most important of sacerdotal studies, and in many monastic orders it is the only study which is seriously cultivated. Young priests have annual examinations in it for many years after their ordination, and throughout life the priest has to attend periodical conferences which are held in every monastery and diocese for the discussion of points of casuistry. Our professor was a young man of much ability and refinement of character, who lectured on the cruder sections with marked confusion and apology, but, as a rule, priests soon acquire the habit of discussing indelicate 'cases' with the calmness of a medical man.

Much as we were attached to our professor for his kindliness and charm of character, we had to procure his removal at the end of a year. Though a man of more than average ability, he was too weak and unsuited for the monastic condition to fill his position with credit.

For our course of dogmatic theology we had the able guidance of Father David. He was a man of wide erudition and considerable mental power, and held us, with one or two exceptions, magnetically bound to him during our studentship. It was a curious fact that nearly all of his students withdrew themselves from his influence in later years. The change seemed to be attributable to the subsequent discovery of the inaccuracy of many of the statements we had taken from him—for want of practice in writing and a shrinking from criticism had encouraged a certain degree of carelessness in his expressions—and partly to the fact that his early kindness and assistance had too much of an element of patronage and authority to survive in maturer years. Personally I was more than usually indebted to his guidance, and I was the last of our course to remain under his influence. Amongst a host of attainments he had a remarkable grasp of dogmatic theology. He had been professor of philosophy in Belgium for many years, and although he was but superficially acquainted with other schools, especially modern schools, he had a profound knowledge of scholastic philosophy, which is the basis of dogmatic theology, and pervades and unites its entire fabric.

For dogmatic theology takes the student in hand at the precise point to which philosophy has conducted him; it is, in fact, merely revelation set in a philosophical framework. The various points of dogma which are contained (or are supposed to be contained) in Scripture, were first selected by the Fathers and developed, generally by the aid of the Neo-Platonic philosophy, into formidable structures. The schoolmen completed the synthesis with the aid of the peripatetic philosophy, and elaborated the whole into a vast scientific scheme which they called Theology. The purely philosophical problems which arose have been extracted, and form the distinct science of metaphysics; the ethical questions have been separated and formed into moral theology; the speculative science which remains, still wholly philosophical in form and largely so in argument, is dogmatic theology.

Dogmatic theology starts with the supposition that the existence and authority of God and the immortality of the human soul—the 'Praeambula fidei,' as they are called—have been rationally proved, with certainty, in philosophy. On these facts, and on the ethical and speculative insufficiency of this 'natural revelation,' it grounds a presumption that a 'positive' revelation has come from behind the veil: from the presumption it proceeds to a demonstration of the historical fact.[1] This is the work of the first treatise or chapter. The second treatise argues for tradition as the organ of revelation (against the Anglicans); the third discusses the constitution of the Church and the prerogatives of the Pope; the fourth is a small but interesting treatise on faith, giving a much more rational explanation of it than an ordinary Catholic is conscious of.

After these fundamental treatises the ground is prepared for argument on supernatural motives: God, the Trinity, the Incarnation, and the Sacraments are discussed in voluminous treatises, and each question is solved by texts of Scripture and quotations from the early Fathers. Scripture and tradition are also confirmed, wherever it is possible, by an argument from reason. It is assumed throughout that every dogma must stand the negative test of reason,

[1] More will be said of this Rationalistic method of Catholic theology, so contrary to common repute, in the last chapter. The author has treated the question more fully in the *Westminster Review*, July 1896.

it must contain no proposition that violates any evident mental law. Hence strenuous efforts are made to ward off the criticism of the Rationalist, and in some cases, as in treating the central point of the Trinitarian dogma or the sacramental presence of Christ in the sacred biscuit, the reasoning becomes curiously subtle and interesting.

Much space, also, is occupied with the conflicts of rival schools of theologians. Thomists (followers of St. Thomas) and Scotists (followers of the Franciscan, Duns Scotus) quarrel religiously on every point of theology that the Church has not defined. The Scotists (Franciscans) are against everybody in everything, for Scotus was the keenest critic that ever kept within the bounds of the Church —a kind of Abelard restrained by profound religious veneration. The Dominicans follow St. Thomas servilely. So do the Jesuits at present, entering, no doubt, into the spirit of their vow of special obedience to the Pope; for Leo XIII. has declared in favour of St. Thomas, and Thomism has spread through the Church like dilettante socialism or a veneration for St. Joachim. The result of the divisions is, that important questions of actual interest are imperfectly grasped by theologians until they find that the world has moved a step, and they then ungracefully follow it: their time is mainly occupied with the thrilling problems of, whether the influence of grace on the soul is physical or moral; whether Christ would still have come upon the earth if Adam had not taken to apples; whether (as it was once put to me) the soul will spend its eternity in careering round the divine essence or in plunging deeper and deeper into it, &c.

Through this scheme of education every student for the Roman Catholic priesthood must pass. In the larger seminaries and more prosperous congregations the programme is carried out with great fidelity, and frequently the more brilliant students are sent, to consolidate and develop their studies, to Louvain University or to Rome. The smaller seminaries and minor congregations, who are ever pressed for priests, curtail the scheme very freely: philosophy is all but omitted, dogmatic theology is reduced to the indispensable minimum, and moral theology is carefully pruned of its luxurious growth of superfluous controversies. In the case of monastic orders whose work consists almost entirely in missionary and parochial activity amongst the poor the Church connives at a lower standard of education.

In the Franciscan Order the constitutions, from which its admirers usually but wrongly derive their information of its practices, generously prescribe three years for philosophy and four for theology. In few branches of the order are more than five years devoted to the higher studies. In England we were the pioneers of a new system, and from first to last our studies were irregular and stunted. We spent five years as students at Forest Gate, of which fifteen months were devoted to classics and rhetoric, fifteen months to philosophy, and two years and a half to theology. During that period our life differed little from the *régime* described in the preceding chapter. We rose at a quarter to five, dragged through the long programme of religious services, and commenced study at eight; six or seven hours per day were devoted to study and the remainder of the time was occupied as has been described.

We had taken the irrevocable vows three years after leaving the novitiate, though, in any case, few of us would have thought of reconsidering our position. All our thoughts went forward in anticipation to the priesthood, the 'finis studiorum,' as we equivocally called it, and we found many means to enliven the dull and insanitary life which must be traversed before reaching it. No vacation was allowed during the whole of the period, but once or twice per week we had the luxury of divesting ourselves of the heavy robe and taking long walks in ordinary clerical costume; once or twice per year, also, we were granted a day trip to some local haunt—when our monastery had tided over its first financial difficulties.

For at the commencement of the period we had ample practical illustration of the meaning of a vow of poverty—which is more than even a mendicant friar really bargains for nowadays. Under one superior, a timid and narrow-minded friar who had been worked into office to serve the purposes of a diplomatic and ambitious higher superior, our diet and clothing became painfully appropriate to our profession of mendicancy; his parsimony and real scarcity of money were neatly concealed behind a cheerful profession and praise of 'holy poverty' before which all complaint was stultified. However, our congregation increased, and the income of the church ran up, so that 'holy poverty' was laid aside in favour of more humane sentiments. Our diet became generous and substantial, our beer and wine more expensive, a heating apparatus was introduced; we almost attained the ordinary level of modern monastic life, and our handsome and comfortable monastery became a significant contrast to the dilapidated cow-shed which had been the first home of the order.

Still the life was extremely insanitary, and there was much sickness amongst us. During three years we lost six of our young men, and almost all of us entered upon our active career with deeply impaired constitutions. Our medical attendant waged a constant but fruitless war with our superiors to procure a saner recreation for us; at his demand for exercise we were furnished with picks and shovels and turned into our garden. One huge mound of earth afforded us exercise for four years; one superior desired to see it in a central heap, his successor fancied it in the form of a Roman camp, and a third directed us to form an intrenchment along the side of the garden with it. But the root of the evil was far deeper than they cared to recognise; it lay in the isolation, the dull, soul-benumbing oppression of the monastic life.

The sick were treated with great kindness, as a rule, but, naturally, with little skill and effectiveness, for no woman is, under any conceivable circumstances, allowed to enter the monastery. In a serious illness which befell me I had acute consciousness of that aspect of celibate life. The custards and beef-tea which the doctor had ordered were made by our cook of corn-flour and somebody's essence of beef (the cook had the laudable intention of saving time for his prayers); and even when certain lady friends outside had taken the responsibility for my diet, I still had the equivocal blessing of 'fraternal' nursing. The lay-brother who acted as my infirmarian, a good, rough, kind-hearted fellow, like most of his class, had been a collier before his conversion, and, though he made a desperate effort to be gentle and soothing, his big horny hands lent themselves very badly to the purpose. However, no expense was spared in the care of the sick, and most superiors were extremely kind and considerate in their treatment.

The constant changes in the *personnel* of the monastery are also one of the forms of relieving the monotony of the life. Elections are held every eighteen months in which changes of superiors are made and religious are transferred from one monastery to another; for months in advance the convents are thrown into a fever of excitement over the issues.

Discontented inferiors are afforded an opportunity of representing their grievances, and they readily submit to harsh treatment in view of the approaching election. In some monasteries and nunneries the superior is elected for life, and in such cases he is chosen by the inmates themselves with great care. In our fraternity the local superiors, or guardians, of the various monasteries were appointed by a higher council,[1] and had to hand in their resignations at the end of eighteen months; when, if their record was satisfactory, they might be re-elected for a time. The frequent change is a matter of general satisfaction, for no superior ever succeeds in gaining the sympathy of an entire community. One of the kindest and ablest superiors we ever had, Father Bede, only retained the position for a year and a half, and at the end of that term was with great difficulty dissuaded from leaving our province altogether. He was a man of exceptionally earnest, active, and respected life; kind, sincere, unworldly, and refined, he is still much honoured in Catholic circles. But the difficulties of office, the petty intrigues of jealous *confrères*, the stupid obstinacy of minor officials, the bitter opposition of a large section of his community, almost drove him from England. One of his colleagues endeavoured to persuade me that F. Bede had only accepted the charge of Forest Gate monastery for the purpose of ruining it; in point of fact he was its warmest and most

---

[1] The election is described more fully p. 178.

effective supporter, and a type of priest whom it is a pleasure to recollect.

Feast-days, also, helped to break the monotony of the life. Even in our poorest days the higher festivals were celebrated with much *éclat*, principally of a gastronomic character; for there are always sufficient thoughtful friends, and usually a nunnery or two, in the neighbourhood of a friary to supply the defects of their masculine cuisine on state occasions. On such days the law of silence is suspended at dinner, and the friars join in a general *mêlée* of conversation and raillery; often, too, an impromptu concert is added, and the songs of by-gone days re-echo through the cloisters. Our refectory was prudently located at the back of the house and far from profane ears. Wine is poured out in abundance; in our days of poverty it was weak Rhine wine or a very suspicious article labelled port, but with the return of prosperity (and the advent of a generous benefactress), good port and whisky and a fair quantity of champagne made their appearance. We students were also liberally supplied with wine, and, as some religiously declined it, others drank copiously.

The long preparation for the priesthood is divided into stages marked by the reception of the preliminary orders. In the Church of Rome there are seven orders through which the cleric must pass, four minor and three major or 'holy' orders. In the early Church each order marked a certain category of officials in which the candidate for the priesthood was detained for some time. The first ceremony, called the 'tonsure,' in which the bishop symbolically cuts five locks of hair from the head of the neophyte, is a formal initiation into the ranks of the clergy; in cutting the hair the bishop repeats the words of the psalm 'Dominus pars hereditatis meae,' for the 'cleric' is one who has thrown in his 'lot' (kleros) with the ministers of the Lord. After a time he passes through the four minor orders and becomes successively doorkeeper, reader, exorcist, and acolythe. Now the tonsure and the minor orders are usually given in one ceremony, for the lower offices have been absorbed into the higher. The inveterate conservatism of the Church of Rome has led to some curious and ridiculous survivals in the ceremony; for instance, after receiving the order of doorkeeper, the cleric is solemnly marched by the master of ceremonies to the church-door, where he pulls the bell, opens the door and shuts it, and returns to the sanctuary for the next step, having 'faithfully discharged his office of doorkeeper.' The function of exorcist can now only be exercised by a priest with the permission of the bishop in each case; in the west of Ireland, where belief in diabolical interference and the power of the priest is still profound and widespread, exorcisms are not unknown.

The subdiaconate is usually received at twenty-one and the diaconate a year afterwards. In the monastic orders, where the vow of celibacy has already been pronounced, these ceremonies are comparatively unimportant, but to the secular student the subdiaconate is a fateful step; the vow is made by taking a step forward in the sanctuary at the invitation of the bishop, and many a student has withdrawn at the last moment. The ceremony of ordination is long and tiresome; it contains many beautiful prayers and much impressive symbolism, but many rites also which are grotesque survivals of former days and much superfluous reading. The bishop reads (generally in a rapid mumbling tone, for they are not now expected to be understood), a series of exhortations to the candidates, who rarely understand a word of his muttered Latin; and, as in the Anglican consecration service, he addresses and interrogates the people present—but, more prudently than his Anglican brother, he does so in the same inaudible Latin.

Two years are supposed to elapse between the diaconate and the priesthood, but we received the three major orders within the same six months. Ecclesiastical laws can always be dispensed by Rome in unusual circumstances, and the extraordinary extent to which clerical regulations are over-ruled and dispensed at the present day gives one the impression that the Church has fallen upon very extraordinary times.

CHAPTER V.

PRIESTHOOD.

A PERUSAL of the scheme of study which has been described would lead to the impression that Roman Catholic priests must be in a highly satisfactory condition of intellectual equipment. No other priesthood has, or ever had, a longer and more systematic course of training. For ten years, on the average, the candidate is under the exclusive control of the ecclesiastical authorities; authorities who have the advantage of an indefinitely long and world-wide experience in training their neophytes and of a religious authority over them. Their scheme of education, indeed, does seem perfectly constructed for the attainment of their particular object.

Yet it is generally recognised that the Catholic priesthood, as a body, are not at all remarkable for their attainments and intellectual training. Their system is admirable on paper, but it evidently breaks down somewhere. That this widely-felt impression of their inferiority is not a lingering deposit of the ancient prejudice against Rome is clear from the fact that Englishmen notice the inferiority more particularly outside of England—where Catholic priests do not present themselves in the light of schismatic intruders. And it is placed beyond all doubt by the circumstance that the feeling is largely and emphatically shared by Catholic [1] laymen. Influential laymen like Dr. Ward and Dr. Mivart have written forcibly on the subject; and, on reading the correspondence columns of Catholic papers, one finds much eagerness amongst the laity for the 'higher education,' not only of women but of the clergy. The broad fact that, with the wider diffusion of recently-acquired knowledge, the theological army has struck its flag and retreated from point after point implies a grave defect even in the intellectual aristocracy of the Church, which does not escape the notice of the layman. It is not, therefore, surprising to find the ordinary clergy much behind the age in questions of general interest.

The last sermon which I preached in a Catholic Church—that of St. Antony at Forest Gate—was an appeal for the higher education of the clergy. I argued that modern thought has entirely changed the position of the religious teacher, and has deeply emphasised the necessity for an intellectual as well as a moral training: and I freely denounced the

---

[1] I make no apology for using the word Catholic as synonymous with Roman. We Romanists felt so proud of the name to which we had clung through the long years when it was a sign of disgrace and persecution that we were loth to part with it.

actual ignorance of the clergy. My mind had already passed from the Roman Catholic faith, and I spoke strongly and sincerely on the subject. My colleagues feebly congratulated me afterwards, but the laymen of the congregation actually sent a deputy to assure me of their gratitude and their admiration of my bold expression of their sentiments. On the following evening, after a scientific lecture I gave them, I spoke on the subject to a group of educated laymen and found them deeply moved on the question. Certainly the clergy of St. Antony's (four of whom were professors) were not below the average. The impression was confirmed wherever one listened to Catholic sermons or entered into serious conversation (by violence) with the priests.

The reasons of this signal failure of a fine educational scheme may be deduced partly from what has preceded. The system is unproductive, in the first instance, on account of the youth and immaturity of the students. At nineteen, when they should still be polishing their wit on Homer, or Tacitus, or Euclid, they are gravely attacking the profoundest problems of metaphysics; a well-educated man of thirty-two who had a brief course of philosophy under F. David, told me that he felt as if he were handling blocks of granite which he fondly wished to penetrate—our usual students never even realised that they were handling 'blocks of granite.' Out of many generations of students who passed through my hands only one boy had an idea of the meaning of philosophy; he confessed to me that it was because, like myself, he was tormented with religious doubt from an early age. Before he reaches the age of twenty-four the student has traversed the whole vast and profound system of scholastic philosophy and theology with its innumerable side-issues and controversies; he has his opinions formed upon every serious subject, and knows what to think of every philosophical and religious system that has ever been invented.

But the studies are not even conducted at the ages and with the intervals prescribed in ecclesiastical legislation; the scarcity of priests (the *raritas vocationum* of which the Pope speaks) induces authorities unduly to accelerate and curtail the course of higher study. Every diocese and nearly every monastic congregation in England is insufficiently manned; thousands of baptized Catholics are wholly neglected for want of priests, and I have known bishops to accept priests who had been practically expelled from other dioceses or congregations. It is true that scores of priests are sent to entertain the natives of Borneo, or bargain with their Anglican brothers over the facetious Ugandians, and that herculean efforts are made to touch the consciences of respectable Anglicans; the fact remains that in East London many thousands of poor Catholics have drifted for want of priests. Pressure and confusion in the seminaries and colleges is the inevitable result.

And it is not merely to procure 'labourers for the vineyard' that the studies are deplorably mutilated; another, and a rather curious, motive of hurry is found in certain congregations at least. Certainly in the Franciscan Order students were prematurely advanced to the priesthood for the sake of earning money by their masses. A mass, of course, cannot be sold; that would be simony. But a priest will say mass for you or your intention if you make him a present of half-a-crown. He may say it gratuitously if he pleases (secular priests generally do, I think), but the bishops have decreed that if a priest accepts a 'stipend' at all he must not take less than half-a-crown; the Church, being socialistic, does not encourage competition. Now every friar is bound to say mass for his superior's intention, and the superior, having to provide for the community, secures as many and as 'fat' stipends as he possibly can. As a friar is bound to say mass every morning he is worth at least 1l. per week on that count alone; in fact, at Forest Gate, where we were six priests, more than 400l. was netted annually in stipends for masses. As a priest, however young he may be, says mass daily from the day of his ordination, the anxiety of the superior to see him ordained appeals to our sympathy; a student is an onus on the community, he must be made productive as soon as possible.

Under such conditions it is not strange that their educational system leads to such unsatisfactory results.

Numbers of young priests are turned out annually upon humanity with full powers to condemn and anathematise, and an intense itching to do so. They soon find that the 'crude and undigested mass' they have 'intussuscepted' is a burden to themselves and a source of pain to their long-suffering audience. In their eagerness to be subtle they teach rank heresy, trouble timid consciences, and hurt themselves against episcopal authority. Then they abandon study entirely, as useless for their purpose. Mr. Jerome has a caricature somewhere of the newly fledged Anglican curate; the young evangelist stands at a table of cigarettes and brandy and soda, and his books are on sale or exchange, 'owner no further use for same.' The skit is wonderfully correct for the average priest.

The canonical age of ordination is twenty-four, and it is, probably, the average age; but this precaution for gravity is nullified by the facility of dispensations. The bishop can dispense at twenty-three, and the Roman authorities readily grant a dispensation once the candidate has reached twenty-two years and two months; most of our friars began to earn their pound per week at the age of twenty-two or three. Under one provincial bishop it is said there was always a brood of half-fledged priests who went by the name of 'Sovereign Pontiffs'; they used to be sent to sing mass on Sundays for priests who were absent or unwell, and the bishop always exacted a 'sovereign' for their services. The usual term of reproach for such immature priests is 'Praesta quaesumus'—an allusion to the fact that they can only say mass, for the expression is a common beginning of mass-prayers.

The ordination is preceded by an episcopal examination in theology. Before the subdiaconate the student must present one treatise on theology for examination; he must prepare two for the diaconate and three for the priesthood. The examination is, however, little more than a test of the memory and industry of the aspirant; if he knows the defined points of Catholic doctrine on the subjects taken, little more is expected of him. And students are usually careful to select the shortest treatises for presentation, and to carry the same treatise through three examinations. Still aspirants are occasionally 'ploughed,' though, judging from the preposterous answers of certain successful students whom I have witnessed at the tribunal, it is difficult to conceive the possibility of failure.

The ceremony of ordination, which may be witnessed on Ember Saturdays in Catholic cathedrals, is very long and highly symbolical. In fact it has developed to such an alarming extent that no theologian can say in what the essence of the ordination really consists: there are innumerable controversies as to which rites are essential to the validity of the 'sacrament.' From the readiness of the theologian to pass judgment on Anglican orders one would imagine that he knew the conditions of validity without hesitation: the truth is that, in each of the three 'sacred orders,' theologians wage ceaseless war over the essentials of ordination. Students are usually in a state of terror about the numerous possibilities of the invalidity of their ordination, and even bishops betray much nervous anxiety in the matter: the ceremony is sometimes repeated for general satisfaction. A curious story is told of a French bishop in illustration of the strange contingencies that affect the validity of orders. He had exercised episcopal functions for many years, when one day his old nurse was heard to boast that she had baptized him, and that she had not used common water for the purpose, but *rose-water*. The baptism was, of course, invalid: his subsequent confirmation and ordination were invalid, for baptism is a condition *sine qua non* of the other sacraments: all the ordinations he had ever held were invalid and had to be repeated—all the masses, absolutions, &c., of himself and his priests had been invalid during that period.

A further source of confusion is found in the necessity of 'jurisdiction' for the validity of certain priestly functions. After ordination he has the power of saying Mass, and no earthly authority can affect its validity: it remains with him until death in every circumstance. On the Catholic theory I still possess that power in full, and if I seriously utter the words *Hoc est enim corpus meum* over the piece of bread I am eating (for that is the essential part of

Mass) it is changed forthwith into the living body of Christ: it is believed on the Continent that apostate priests frequently consecrate for the Satanists and Freemasons. However the power of absolving from sin is not of the same character; it is only radically received in the ceremony of ordination, and the validity of its exercise is entirely dependent upon ecclesiastical authority. M. Zola, most patient and accurate of inquirers, has overlooked this distinction; in 'Lourdes' the Abbé Pierre is made to hear Marie's confession when he has no jurisdiction over her and could not validly absolve her.[1]

A second examination (in casuistry) is necessary before 'faculties' to hear confessions are granted, which is usually some time after ordination. And jurisdiction is limited to the diocese of the bishop who gives faculties, and may be still further restricted at his pleasure: nunneries and boarding-schools are always excepted from it; and there are always a certain number of sins which the bishop reserves for himself. In some dioceses (Kerry, for instance) the list of 'reserved cases' is long and interesting: it usually comprises the sins which are most prevalent in a district—perjury for instance, is reserved in Kerry,

---

[1] A non-Catholic writer is almost certain to stumble in liturgical matters. M. Zola's administration of the sacraments to the dying— to the pilgrim in the train, in 'Lourdes,' and to Count Dario in 'Rome'—is quite incorrect. It has never been pointed out, too, that the moon's conduct, during Pierre's three last nights in Rome, is out of all bounds of astronomical propriety.

for it is as common as truth in a court of justice. The confessor, in such cases, has to write to the bishop for absolution, and tell his penitent to return to him. In London four cases are reserved: immoral advances by a priest to a woman in the confessional, frequentation of theatres by a priest, murder, and connection with a secret society. Two cases which are always reserved to the Pope will be treated in the next chapter.

For a long period after his ordination the priest's activity is confined to saying Mass every morning. He is not indeed bound to say Mass every morning:[1] he is bound to *hear* Mass every Sunday, but there is no definite obligation to exercise his power of consecration. The young priest says it daily during the few years of his primitive fervour, and many priests continue the practice faithfully throughout life. Monastic priests are usually bound to say daily mass by their constitutions, though there is no doubt that it would be much more conducive to true religion if they were allowed liberty of choice. Priests soon contract the habit of hurrying through their Mass at a speed which ill harmonises with their belief in its most solemn character. In fact, the Church has been forced to legislate on the point and forbid the saying of Mass in less than twenty minutes—or fifteen

[1] M. Zola is again wrong in imputing it as a fault that the priests at Lourdes omitted to say Mass.

minutes for a 'black' Mass.¹ No doubt a priest works up to a high rate of speed largely out of anxiety to meet the wishes of his congregation, yet the sight is distressing to one who knows how much is squeezed into the twenty minutes. An ordinary worshipper merely sees the rapid irreverent genuflections and the desperate hand movements which are supposed to be reverent crosses over the sacrament, but the mutilation of the prayers is much more deplorable: nearly all are direct and more or less familiar petitions to the Almighty, and one cannot but fondly hope (for the priest's sake) that he is wholly unconscious of the meaning of his orisons. It is difficult, no doubt, when a large congregation is shifting uneasily on the benches, and perhaps another priest is frowning upon you from the chancel, waiting for his turn. Certainly there are very many priests who acquit themselves with edifying devotion, but the majority run through their Mass (apart from pressure) in the allotted twenty minutes; and, since it takes a priest nearly an hour to say Mass in his early practising days, one can imagine at what price the high speed is obtained.

The Mass is rendered rather ludicrous sometimes from an opposite reason—through its undue prolonga-

---

[1] A black Mass—in which the priest wears black vestments—is shorter than usual: hence it is that black vestments so often adorn the shoulders of an ordinary secular priest. Green vestments are worn on a common, saintless day; red for a martyr or the Holy Ghost; white for virgins, confessors and all great feasts; purple for sadder festivals; and gold for any purpose.

tion and interruption by musical accompaniment. The High Mass only differs from the daily Low Mass in the number of assistants and the musical rendering. It is supremely incongruous, from a purely religious point of view, for the celebrant to interrupt his solemn rites whilst he and his congregation listen to the florid strains of Haydn or Gounod, operatically rendered by soulless singers who have no idea of the meaning of their words, and are very frequently non-Catholics. Leo XIII. did make an effort in the direction of reform, but he must have realised that it is the *éclat* of the ceremony which fills Catholic churches all the world over, not the mysterious and unintelligible Mass.

At the same time it must be said that the Church does not do all in its power to make the Mass (and other ceremonies) appeal to the priest. In its stolid conservatism it retains a number of vestments, rites, &c., which have become absolutely unmeaning. The humeral veil, which is worn by the subdeacon at Mass and by the priest at benediction, is an undignified survival of the once intelligible custom of drawing a veil across the sanctuary and at the most solemn moments; the maniple, an embroidered cloth that dangles at the priest's left elbow, is not only unmeaning but gravely inconvenient. The practice of solemnly facing the people to sing the epistle and gospel *in Latin*, and other such survivals of early custom, are interesting from an archæological point of view, but ought to have been changed centuries ago; indeed, no serious defence can be made of the use of Latin at all in the Church of Rome.

Ecclesiastical Latin is, of course, easy, still it is a fact that many priests know so little Latin of any kind that many parts of the Mass and Office are quite hieroglyphic to them. I remember a country priest who was invited to bless a churn. He took the book of (Latin) benedictions to the farm, and donned his surplice; not knowing the Latin for a churn (which may be excused) he pitched upon a 'Benedictio thalami' as probably referring to a churn, and read the 'Blessing of a marriage bed' with the usual solemnity over the churn of cream.[1] Certainly some of the sequences in the Mass and many of the hymns in the Breviary are beyond the capacity of a large number of priests.

And it must be admitted that no familiarity with Latin will enable the priest to attach a meaning to certain portions of the liturgy—especially to some of the psalms. The approved Latin version of the Psalter is a disgraceful performance; yet it has been used for

[1] There are blessings for every thing conceivable. In my younger days a woman once asked me to read a prayer over her; I could not divine the particular purpose and she seemed uncommunicative. So I chose one, rather at random; she was safely delivered of twins shortly afterwards. In Belgium I was much tormented for sending a young woman, who came to me with a severe tooth-ache, to a dentist, and an old lady, who had diseased cows, to a veterinary surgeon. I incurred grave suspicions of rationalism from my colleagues.

1,600 years, and there is no question of changing it. St. Jerome, an expert Hebraist, offered an excellent translation in his classical Latin, but the monks knew the old Psalter by heart and would not change; hence the first translation of the psalms, into bad Latin by very imperfect Hebrew scholars, endures to this day. Some of the psalms—notably the 58th—contain unmitigated absurdities; the verse 'Kings of armies have fled, have fled' is rendered, 'King of virtues, beloved, beloved'; verse 13 runs, 'If you sleep in the middle of the lots, the wings of the dove are silvered,' &c. There are many similar verses. Yet the good old monks, who doubtless found many deep symbolical meanings in the above, clung to the version, and their modern successors may be excused for wool-gathering during their chanting.

For about forty psalms enter into the daily 'Office' which the priest has to recite. One often sees a secular priest mumbling over his Breviary in train or omnibus; he is bound to form the words with his lips, at least. The monks, however, recite their Office in their choir, or private chapel, which is fitted like the stalls of a cathedral. The two sides take up the alternate verses of the psalms, chanting the words in a loud monotone; it is only sung on solemn occasions. The whole of it is set to music, and in such inactive monasteries as the Carthusians, where it is a question what to do with one's time, the whole is sung daily.

It takes about three hours to chant it in the ordinary monotone, and no normal human being could continue in real prayer so long. Indeed, the facility with which the solemn rows of chanting friars could be thrown into fits of laughter gave little token of their great earnestness. Incidents abounded and were highly appreciated. In Killarney we had a priest who read the prayers so furiously that he invariably got inextricably wrapped up in them and threw us novices into convulsions. At London, one day, our instructor, who led one side of the choir, suddenly raised the tone about an octave in the middle of the psalm. The head superior, who led the other side, disagreed with him (as usual); we were afraid to join with either, for they were both equally formidable to us, so we listened with interest as they continued the psalm to the end, chanting alternate verses at a distance of an octave and a half.

There was an asterisk, too, in the middle of each verse which occasioned much distraction; one of our friars received the permanent title of 'The star' in connection with it. F. Cuthbert, an amiable and excellent old friar, was superior of the small friary at Stratford; one member of the community was a stone-deaf old friar who had naturally dropped into the habit of going straight ahead with his share of the chanting, in sweet unconsciousness of the doings of his colleagues. As he paid little or no attention to the asterisk—which was a signal for pause—he was repeatedly called to order by F. Cuthbert shouting 'The star, the star!' in his ear.

And if there was much to be desired in these religious offices which were of a private character it will be readily imagined that their public services were not more satisfactory. During the long hours which monks and nuns devote to prayer every day it is impossible to expect a continuous ecstasy on their part; and, since most of the psalms do not vary from day to day, the very monotony of the services would stand in the way of any very serious devotion. But in their public ceremonies another distracting element is introduced, the presence of closely observant spectators; it were not in human nature to be insensible of their presence. The sanctuary becomes a stage, and strive how he may to think of higher things, the ordinary mortal cannot banish the thought that some hundreds, perhaps thousands, of eyes are bent upon his every movement; the Catholic sanctuary with its myriads of burning tapers, its fragrant incense, its glory of colour in flowers and vestments, compels attention—every line of the church converges towards the tabernacle, the priest.

Hence it is not surprising to find that there is a vast amount of empty formalism and purely dramatic effect in sanctuary work. One cannot, of course, attach much importance to the grave and devout expressions of the ministers, for it is part of their discipline: from their earliest years they have been accustomed to a close supervision from superiors, and in the course of time the countenance comes to adapt itself automatically to the occupation. In point of fact there are few who are not keenly concerned about the material success of their function—their singing, their deportment and appearance. At such a time as Holy Week, for instance, the feverish anxiety for the success of the extraordinary services runs so high that one may safely say they are quite unattended with religious feeling in the sanctuary: ceremonies and music are practised for weeks in advance, and, when the time comes, celebrants are too busy and too nervous to think of more than the merely mechanical or theatrical part of the devotions.

And the same thought applies, naturally, to preaching: it runs on the same lines in the Church of Rome as in every other church. There are deeply religious preachers whose only serious thought is for the good of their hearers, as they conceive it; there are preachers who think only of making a flattering impression on their audience, or who are utterly indifferent what effect or impression they produce: the vast majority strive to benefit their hearers, and are not unassisted in their efforts by a very natural modicum of self-interest. I heard a typical story of one a few years ago. The priest in question is one of the most familiar figures in Catholic circles in the north of England, an ardent zealot for the 'conversion' of England, and, I believe, a very earnest and worthy man. On this occasion he was preaching in the open air to a large special congregation who had made a pilgrimage to the ancient home of one of the priests who had come to grief for political misfortunes under Elizabeth. The preacher was eloquent, carried away, apparently, by his feelings on the subject. My informant, however, a keen critic of elocution, noticed that one gesture—a graceful sweep of the wide-sleeved arm—was unduly prolonged, and, looking more closely, he saw that the preacher was signalling to a photographer in the opposite corner of the quadrangle. The preacher told him afterwards that he had arranged to be photographed at this specially prepared gesture. The photographer had been so captivated by the sermon that he had to be recalled to a sense of duty by the perfervid orator himself.

I remember in my younger days being grievously shocked at one of the London 'stars.' I happened to be near the door when he re-entered the cloister after an unusually fervent discourse, and he immediately burst out with the exclamation: 'Now, where is that port you promised me!' Five years afterwards I used to feel grateful myself for a glass of port after preaching: it is not apostolic, but this is not an apostolic age, and only merits contempt when it professes to be one.

If the priest has an educated congregation he usually prepares his sermon with care. The sermons are rarely original, for there is a vast library of *sermonnaires* at the disposal of the Catholic priest, but it is often written out in full, though it is never read from the pulpit, as is done in Anglican congregations. Good preaching is, however, rather the exception than the rule: though the age of martyrs has passed away, a Catholic can always find a sufficient test of his faith in the shape of an indifferent preacher who insists on thinking that he needs two three-quarters of an hour sermons every Sunday. In poor parishes the sermons usually degenerate into intolerable harangues. A priest who had charge of a large poor mission told me that he always prepared his sermon the hour before it was delivered: he took a cup of tea, lit a cigar, opened the gospel of the day and thought dreamily over it, then he ascended the pulpit and preached for half an hour. Men of wide erudition and facility of utterance, like F. David, would often preach most impressive sermons at a few minutes' notice; others, of the type of Canon Akers and F. Bede, an ascetic, earnest, contemplative type, would also preach sound and rational moral discourses without preparation. The practice of preaching the same sermon many times is, of course, widely prevalent. I remember one old friar fondly kissing a much worn manuscript after a sermon on St. Joseph: 'God bless it,' he said, 'that is the sixty-third time I have preached it.'

There are many other functions in which the priest finds it difficult to sustain the becoming attitude:

confession will be treated in the next chapter; extreme unction is a ceremony in which only a keen faith, keener than usually flourishes in the nineteenth century, can take a religious interest. But it is in the ceremony of baptism, especially, that the most unreasonable rites survive and the most diverting incidents occur. There is a long series of questions to be put to the sponsors, and the Church, unmindful apparently of the march of time, still insists on their being put in Latin and repeated afterwards in English. One lay-brother who used to assist me in baptising thought it more proper for him to learn the Latin responses instead of allowing me to answer myself; unfortunately he muddled the dialogues, and to my query: 'Dost thou believe in God the Father, &c.?' he answered, with proud emphasis, 'I renounce him.'

In point of fact, however, I was little occupied with sacerdotal functions. Even before my ordination I had been appointed to the chair of Philosophy, and as soon as I became a priest I entered upon the duties of professor. My application to that science had been noticed by our authorities, and probably attributed to a natural taste for the subject. The truth was I had fallen upon a period of acute religious scepticism, and I knew that philosophy alone could furnish the answer to my doubts, if such answer were obtainable. My misgiving had commenced six years previously, in the novitiate, and I had duly confessed my state of mind to my superior. Kind and earnest as he was, he had nevertheless little capacity for such emergencies ; he made me kneel at his feet in his cell and, after plying me for a long time with a sort of 'argumentum ad verecundiam '—holding up the exemplary faith of Wiseman, Newman, &c.—he discharged me with the usual admonition to stifle immediately any further temptation of that character. He acted upon the received ascetical principle that there are two kinds of temptations which must be fled from, not met and fought, namely, temptations against purity and temptations against faith : in the second case the rule is certainly dishonest, and sheds much light upon the position of many clergymen. Indeed, thoughtful priests do not recognise it, though it is sanctioned, in theory and practice, by the majority.

My scepticism increased : it was partly the effect of temperament, partly a natural desire to verify the opinions which I found myself acting upon. At London I immediately put myself under the guidance of F. David, and for seven years he was informed, almost weekly, of the growth of my thoughts. Though most intimate with him I never allowed him to make any allusion to my difficulties outside the confessional, but, in confession, I spent many hours propounding my difficulties and listening with profound attention to his replies. As time went on I began to feel that I had exhausted his apologetical resources, that he had but the old thread-bare formulæ to oppose to my ever-deepening difficulties: I was, therefore, more dependent upon my own studies, and, as my difficulties were wholly philosophical, I devoted myself with untiring energy to the study of scholastic philosophy. If, in later years, I did not appeal to F. David when the crisis came, it was because I was firmly convinced that I had, in private and in public lectures, heard all that he had to say on the subject. He was the only man who knew that my secession was not the work of one day, but the final step in a bitter conflict of ten long painful years. All that my *confrères* knew was that I was ever reticent and gloomy (which was, I think, attributed to pride and to sickness), and that I was strangely enamoured of metaphysics: I was accordingly appointed professor of that subject.

In due time I received jurisdiction and commenced the full exercise of sacerdotal power. A monastic superior has the power of examining his own subjects, and thus practically dispensing with the episcopal examinations. Knowing that I was not a zealous student of casuistry F. David kindly undertook my examination: he asked me the formula of absolution (which I did not know) one day when I met him in the cloister, and then sent me up to the Vicar General as 'examined and found worthy.' The late Bishop Weathers used to give candidates for jurisdiction a long and conscientious examination, but the young priests soon found out his vulnerable point. When the examination had proceeded a little they would ask his advice on one of his pet subjects, and a good hour of the time would be usefully occupied to their mutual satisfaction. I then immediately entered the mysterious and much dreaded confessional. Preaching and other functions also commenced, and I was now fully launched in my sacerdotal career.

CHAPTER VI

THE CONFESSIONAL

No point in the vast and much contested system of the Church of Rome has excited, and still excites, a deeper and a more suspicious interest than the practice of auricular confession. The Inquisition and the commerce in relics[1] and indulgences are still favourite subjects of the historical critic; monasticism, the Index, the dead language, political ambition and intrigue are some of its actual features which attract no small quantity of opprobrium, and even try the patience of many of its own adherents. But the happy hunting-ground of the innumerable tribe of anti-papal lecturers and pamphleteers is the confessional. Unlike monastic life, the air of mystery and secrecy is a necessary evil of the confessional, and it is the characteristic which is most incentive to criticism. A Catholic layman cannot, of course, with delicacy enlarge upon his experience of the confessional, and, in any case, it would be too personal to be instructive or effective. No ex-priest has hitherto given his

---

[1] Though this practice has not yet become extinct (see *postea*, p. 191).

impressions of the institution; no priest would venture to express an unfavourable opinion upon it, or even any opinion of a circumstantial character, for fear of alarming his co-religionists.

Yet in point of fact there is no reason in the nature of things why even an actual confessor should not write a most ample and detailed account of his experiences. The 'seal of confession' is not merely a sacramental obligation, it is a natural obligation which no ex-priest would ever dream of violating. But the obligation has certain limits which are explicitly defined in theological works and are practically observed by priests. The obligation is merely to maintain such secrecy about confessional matters as shall prevent the knowledge of the crime of *a definite individual*: within those limits the obligation is absolute and admits of no possible excuse in the smallest matter. The priest is not even allowed to use a probability in his own favour in this question: he is forbidden under an obligation of the gravest possible character to say a single word or perform any action whatever from which the declaration of his penitent might possibly be inferred. Hence he cannot, under any conceivable circumstances, act upon the information he has received. If a priest learned from the confession of his servant that she had put poison in the wine he was to take for dinner, Catholic theology directs that he must not even change the bottle, but act precisely as if he had heard nothing. I never heard of a test case, though it is well known that there have been martyrs to the seal of confession. In minor matters, of course, the confessor interprets his obligation generously. One of our friars, the superior of a monastery, interrupted an inferior who was confessing to him, made him stand up and repeat *extra sigillum*, a certain fault for which he wished to inflict a public penance: it was a breach of the seal, though my colleague was too subtle a casuist to admit it. I remember a priest who was confessor to an acquaintance of mine once saying to me of her: 'Miss —— seems to be a very well educated person, she speaks quite smoothly on the most delicate points.' I doubt whether my friend would have cared for me to know so much of her confession.

However, once the danger of identifying the individual concerned is precluded, the confessor is free to make whatever use he pleases of his acquired knowledge. It is added in theological works that it is extremely imprudent to discuss such matters before seculars, but that is only part of the *economia* of the priest with regard to the laity, not a moral obligation. And amongst themselves priests discuss their interesting experiences very freely; the professor of casuistry is usually a man of wide experience who gives his students the full benefit thereof. In their conferences they are most generous with their experiences. To discuss the relative wickedness of town and country, of large cities, of localities in a city is a common practice of missionaries. Such commentaries, however, are carefully restricted to sacerdotal circles: there is no doubt that any departure from the policy of unqualified secrecy would deeply impair the fidelity of the laity, and tend to withdraw them from that greatest focus of sacerdotal influence, the confessional.

And there is another reason why confessors have not thought it necessary to enter into the controversy to any important extent. The attacks upon the confessional have usually defeated their own object by emphasizing too strongly the accidental rather than the inherent and essential evil of the institution. Dark stories—which may quite possibly be true as exceptional cases—are circulated in connection with it, and the impression is at once urged that such practices are a normal, or at least a large, part of what is hidden under the veil of secrecy. The generalisation is fatal, for the Catholic apologist has little difficulty in pointing out the impossibility of such a state of things; besides, the days are happily gone by when the Catholic priesthood as a body could be accused of systematic and conscious immorality. The main contention of the critic having been thus met and answered, attention is diverted from the real evil of the confessional, which is not sufficiently realised by those who are unfamiliar with it.

The structures which are found in every Catholic

church for the purpose of hearing confessions are quite exclusive of such an opinion. The penitent usually remains in sight of the congregation, and, in any case, priest and penitent are not in the same compartment: a wire gauze-work, set into the partition, enables them to talk in whispers, but contact is impossible. These 'boxes' or confessionals are open for inspection in any church. In hearing the confessions of nuns the precautions are still more stringent, as a rule; the confessor is enclosed in a kind of *bureau*, the nun remaining entirely outside.

One circumstance, however, should not be overlooked: it is, that the priest is not bound to hear every confession in the 'box,' and that he frequently hears them in less guarded places. Indeed, I have heard the confessions of a whole community of nuns where no such precautions existed: they entered singly and entirely unobserved into the room where I sat to hear them. Their usual confessor was a venerable and harmless old priest, and it was not thought necessary to alter the arrangements for me. During certain hours on Saturday, the priest sits in his box for all comers: outside those hours he will hear confessions in the sacristy or anywhere, and the anti-papal lecturer may find legitimate food for reflection in that section of his practice.

Confessions are also frequently heard at the private houses of the penitents. The Church does not sanction the practice with regard to people who are capable of attending church, but it is frequently necessary to hear the confessions of persons who are confined to bed. The priest is urged, in such cases, to leave doors open and take various precautions to avoid scandal, but those directions are seldom acted upon and would not be appreciated, as a rule, by the penitent herself. Cases are not unknown in which women have feigned or exaggerated illness for that purpose. But such appointments are attended with great danger, and cannot be widespread.

Indeed, I do not believe that there is any unusual amount of immorality in connection with the confessional; rather the reverse, for the legislation of the Church on that point is stringent and effective, and the priest is well aware that the confessional is the worst place in the world for him to indulge improper tendencies. He is involved in a network of regulations, and sooner or later his misconduct is bound to come to the knowledge of his authorities, with very disastrous consequences to himself. In the first place, as I explained in the last chapter, improper suggestion on the part of the confessor is a sin reserved to the bishop. He cannot say Mass until he has received absolution (for it is assumed that he has not lost all sense of obligation[1]) and no brother priest can absolve

---

[1] In that case his infidelity might not be revealed until death, when any priest can absolve. A curious case was mentioned (by a priest) in the *Daily Telegraph* a few years ago. At the death of a Catholic military chaplain a woman presented herself to the army authorities as his wife, and actually produced a certificate to that effect.

him from his fault: he must have recourse to the bishop, and it is safe to presume that he will not relapse for a considerable period. In the second place he is deprived of the power of absolving his accomplice—an attempt to do so is a sin reserved to the Pope, and, as every woman knows that such absolution is invalid, the misconduct is once more liable to come to the cognizance of the authorities. The second sin which is reserved to the Pope is a false denunciation of a confessor by a woman, so that one has a guarantee of the genuineness of such denunciations as are actually made.

Thus it is obviously ill-advised for the unfaithful priest to make an evil use of the confessional, for the danger of exposure is sternly prohibitive. A devout Roman Catholic is horrified at the very speculation; an impartial thinker, whose estimate of human nature is neither unduly raised by thoughts of special graces nor depressed by prejudice, will think of priests as men more than usually exposed to temptation and handicapped with an enforced celibacy, but will give them credit, on the whole, for an honest effort to realise that higher integrity which they profess. He will not think them *superhuman* with the Catholic, nor *infrahuman* with the ultra-Protestant: he will not believe that any of their habitual practices are inherently immoral, but he will expect the occasional lapses which no large body of men can prevent. And he will be perfectly right.

The danger of the priest is not in the confessional, it is the same as for any voluntary celibate, and need not be enlarged upon; though it must be remembered that, in the light of what has been said about the age of taking the vow, the priest must be regarded practically as an *involuntary* celibate. The fact that from time immemorial ecclesiastical legislation has returned again and again to the question of priests' servants is significant enough. The house to house visits of the priests, and the visits he receives, are also principally of ladies, for the priest is idle in the hours that the husband is employed. Priests are, however, as a rule, extremely cautious in this regard.

Whatever may be said of the general integrity of the priest's life it may be safely admitted that the occasional transgressions of his vow in connection with the confessional have been grossly exaggerated. And one unfortunate feature of the excess is that it has withdrawn attention from the essential hideousness of the 'tribunal of penance.' For in point of fact nothing could be more degrading, to priest and penitent alike, than the practice of auricular confession. It is bad enough for adult men and women to have to kneel weekly or monthly at the feet of a priest (usually one whom they know intimately), and detail every unworthy thought and act into which they have been betrayed, but for girls and young women to discuss their inmost thoughts and feelings with a person of the opposite sex, is vicious and lamentable. If they are still of a refined character such a practice is a source of exquisite pain, and often leads either to duplicity or to actual debasement; if they are less refined already the temptation to abuse their condition is overpowering.

When I first began to hear confession I was much impressed with the number of girls who unburdened their minds to me (I was practically a stranger to them) on some long-concealed transgression of an indelicate character. A Catholic girl usually selects a particular confessor (we were six in number at Forest Gate) and presents herself at his box every week, fortnight, or month. The priest learns to recognise her voice, if he does not know her already, and counts her amongst his regular penitents, of which every confessor is proud to possess a certain number. Week after week she comes with her small catalogue of the usual feminine maladies — fibs, tempers, and slanders — at last she is betrayed into some graver fault, or something she imagines, generally after it has taken place, to be serious. If she goes to another confessor her habitual director will know it, for she is bound to say how long it is since her last confession : he will in all probability form his own opinion on the matter—some confessors do not scruple to exact a repetition of the confession to themselves. To him, she is often quite unable to confess it after her long immunity from evil in his esteem; she therefore conceals, and continues her confessions and communions for months, even years, without confessing it. Now each such confession and communion, she has been taught, is as vile a sin as murder or adultery. She goes through life with her soul in her hands and the awful picture of a Catholic hell burning deeper into her; until at last, in an agony of fear, she crouches one day in the corner of the box and falters out the dread secret of her breaking heart. And it must be remembered that the subject of so much pain is often no real sin at all. The most unavoidable feelings and acts are confused with the most pernicious practices, and often regarded as 'mortal sins.'

But a yet sadder category is the large number of girls who are actually corrupted by the practice of confession. Girls who would never dream of talking to their companions, even to their sisters or mothers, on certain points will talk without the least restraint to the priest. They are taught when young that such is the intention of Christ, that in the confessional every irregular movement (and to their vaguely disciplined moral sense the category embraces the whole of sexual physiology) must be revealed: they are reminded that nothing superfluous must be added, still that the sense of shame in the confessional must be regarded as a grave temptation of the evil one. So they learn to control it, then to lay it aside temporarily, and finally to lose it. They begin to confer with each other on the subject, to compare the impressibility, the inquisitiveness, the knowledge of different confessors, and make plots (they have admitted so much to me) to put embarrassing questions to priests.

For, although they frequently manifest a quick sense of shame and delicacy at the commencing period they are forced to be more circumstantial in their narratives. A girl will often try to fit in her less delicate transgressions between two common and more respectable peccadilloes, and only accuse herself in a general way of having been 'rude,' or immodest. No confessor can allow such a general accusation to pass: he is bound to recall her and question her minutely on the subject. The conversation which ensues is much better imagined than described; for by some curious process of reasoning (assisted by the light of faith) the Church of Rome has deduced from certain words of Christ that the confessor must have a detailed knowledge of every serious transgression before he can give absolution.

Finally, there is a still more curious and pitiable category of victims of the sacrament of penance. A missionary priest who travels from parish to parish is often warned that he will get certain women to confession who must be handled very carefully; they are practically monomaniacs of the system, and are found in many parishes in London. Sometimes they have a mania for denouncing priests to the bishop for solicitation, and in the hope of getting evidence they will entangle him in the crudest conversation.

Sometimes they are women 'with a history,' which, in their morbid love of the secret conversation, they urge, freshly varnished and redecorated, upon every confessor they meet, and make him think that he has secured a Magdalen; frequently they are embryo novelists who deliberately concoct the most shameless stories in order to gratify their craving for that peculiar *tête-à-tête* which they have grown accustomed to in the confessional.

This, then, is the essential, inalienable evil of the confessional. It may not be so directly productive of gross acts as is frequently supposed, but it has a corrosive, corruptive influence that marks it out as an object of horror to all save those who have been familiar with it from childhood. And yet this system, of so grave a responsibility, has the most slender basis of all the institutions of the Church of Rome. The reasoning by which it is deduced from Scripture is a masterpiece of subtlety—certainly 'unaided' reason could not have achieved it. 'Whose sins ye shall forgive they are forgiven, and whose sins ye shall retain they are retained,' is the sole text bearing on the subject: the Catholic method of inferring the *obligation* of confession from the latter part of the text is interesting, and yet very simple. The apostles have the power of retaining sin: if it were possible to obtain forgiveness in any other way than by absolution from the apostles or their successors the power of retaining sin would be nugatory; therefore there is only one way of obtaining forgiveness—by absolution, after full confession. This argument is strengthened by another powerful one from tradition, from the fact that, in the fourth century, the Church claimed, against the Novatians, the power of absolving from all sins; but what was meant in the fourth century by confession and absolution is not quite clear even to Catholic theologians, and an outsider may be excused for not seeing the force of the argument.

The fact is that, when the Church first began (in the thirteenth century) to talk about the obligation of confession, it had not the same rationalistic spirit to face which it has to-day. It found that a practice had somehow developed amongst the faithful which could be utilised as a most powerful lever, and it proceeded to make the practice obligatory: the newly founded religious orders were administering their spiritual narcotics to humanity, and the law was accepted with docility. Hence, in our own days, when the Church must provide a more rational basis for its tenets and institutions, the search for proofs of the divine institution of the practice is found to be more than usually difficult to the expert interpreters of the Church of Rome.

Apart, however, from its feeble dogmatic defence it is usual for preachers and writers to expatiate upon the moral advantages of the practice; sermons on the subject are conspicuously frequent, for it is well known that many Anglicans are deterred by it from passing over to Rome. One of our most powerful preachers at Forest Gate gave a course of sermons on the confessional for the avowed purpose of 'converting' a non-Catholic solicitor who attended our Church, and who was thought to be deterred by the confessional. It is urged that confession gives a certain relief to the soul burdened with the consciousness of sin—which, in the majority of cases, is the reverse of the truth, and in any case does not touch the question of obligatory confession; and especially the confessional is lauded as a great preventive of sin. Whatever may be thought of the intrinsic probability of such an issue (which the preacher exclusively regards) we must candidly admit that, in the estimation of the community at large, Catholics are neither more nor less moral than their fellow-countrymen. To compare Catholic countries against Protestant would be fruitless and unprofitable: there is not a country or city in the civilised world which has not its distinguished advocates for the title of 'the most immoral.' London, Christiania, and Berlin, if we must strike an average of opinions, are neither better nor worse than Paris, Rome, or Madrid. But within our own frontiers there is a large section of frequenters of the confessional, and a comparison of their average lives with those of their fellow citizens reflects no special credit upon their institutions as moral prophylactics. Liverpool and Glasgow are much more Catholic than Manchester or London:

missionaries admit that they are much more immoral —setting apart the Parisian immorality of West London of which the missionary is blissfully ignorant.

'And, indeed, the confessional does not exercise any general restraining influence upon its frequenters. No doubt a priest is often able to exert a good influence over his habitual penitent, but, on the other hand, large numbers of young people are encouraged in vice by the facility of absolution. I have been informed by penitents, on more than one occasion, that they have sinned *more readily* under the influence of the thought of confession. In certain monastic or quasi-monastic institutions the weekly confession to the chaplain does exercise a certain degree of influence, but even here nature has its revenge. The temptation to conceal and the practice of concealing is so great that the Church commands the introduction of an extraordinary confessor every three months, and commands each monk or nun or cleric to present himself: in discharging that function I have not only met cases of long concealment, as might be expected, but I have known them to deliberately indulge their morbid tendencies in the prospect of my coming. I have heard confessions in very many parts of England and abroad, I have read much casuistic literature which is permeated with confessional experience, and I have conferred on the subject with missionaries who have heard hundreds of thousands of confessions; and I am convinced that the majority of Catholics are unaffected by the confessional. They are bound to confess once every year; if they wish to pass as men of ordinary piety they confess every month or oftener; but in the whirligig of life the confessional is forgotten and has no influence whatever on their morality.

That the institution is a source of great power to the Church at large is easily understood: it creates a vast gulf between clergy and laity, and considerably accentuates the superiority of the former. But to the large number of individual priests the function is, naturally, very distasteful. Apart from the obvious unpleasantness of the task it is much more fatiguing than would be supposed. Three or four hours continuous hearing I have found very exhausting, and a missionary has frequently to spend seven or eight hours per day in the box. Still there are many priests who manifest a positive predilection for the work, and they will sit for hours in their boxes waiting—one could not help comparing them to patient spiders—for the arrival of penitents.

The obligation of confessing commences at the age of seven years and is incumbent upon every member of the Church, clergy and laity alike, even on the pope, who has a simple harmless Franciscan friar serving him in that capacity. The theory is that the obligation of confessing commences when the possibility of contracting grave sin is first developed, and in the eyes of the Church of Rome the average child of seven is capable of meriting eternal damnation by its acts. Needless to say, the confession of the average child of seven or eight is a mere farce: they used to be marched over to us from the schools every three months, after a careful drilling from their teachers, but scarcely one child in ten had the faintest glimmering of an idea of the nature of the operation they were subjected to. Few of them could even be sufficiently instructed to fulfil the material part of the ceremony: they mixed the various parts of the formulæ in the most unintelligible fashion, and generally wished to retreat before they had received the essential object of their coming—absolution.

The method of the ceremony is described in any Roman Catholic prayer book. The penitent first kneels for ten or fifteen minutes in the church and, with the aid of the minute catalogue of sins in his book, recalls his transgressions since his last confession. Entering the box, and usually asking the priest's blessing, he states the occasion of his last confession, so that the confessor may form a correct estimate of his sinfulness. He then states his faults, the number of times he has committed each, and any aggravating circumstances; if the confessor is not satisfied he questions him and elicits further details. Then premising, as a rule, a few words of exhortation or reproof, he imposes a penance and dismisses him with absolution, after an act of sorrow and a promise to amend. It is hardly necessary to add, in these enlightened days, that no money is ever exacted or received for absolution: the stories circulated by certain clerical travellers of lists of prices of absolution seen in Continental churches are entirely devoid of foundation—if any lists existed outside their heated imaginations they were probably lists of prices of chairs or of votive candles. It may be added, too, that an 'indulgence' has no reference whatever to future sin, but is a remission of purgatorial punishment due to sin, *already forgiven*, which the Church of Rome believes herself empowered to give. That indulgences are still practically sold cannot be denied for a moment: not that a written indulgence is now ever handed over for so much hard cash—such bargains have proved too disastrous to the Church—but papal blessings, richly indulgenced crosses and rosaries, &c., are well known rewards of the generous almsgiver.

A curious instance is mentioned in Dr. Tyndall's 'Sound' of a church in which certain acoustic peculiarities enable the listener at a distant point to hear the whispers in the confessional: it is said that a husband had the equivocal pleasure of hearing his own wife's confession. Such contingencies are foreseen and provided for in theological works: the seal of confession applies not only to the priest, but to every person who comes to a knowledge of confessional matter. Indeed, it happens not infrequently that the penitents waiting outside overhear the words of priest or penitent, especially when one or other is a little deaf. At a church in Manchester one busy Saturday evening the priest interrupted his labours to inquire the object of a scuffle outside his box. As usual there was a quarrel about precedence amongst the mixed crowd that waited their turn at the door. A boy was complaining of being deprived of his legitimate place, and when the priest's head appeared he appealed to him with the startling intelligence: 'Please, father, I was next to the woman who stole the silk umbrella!' And in my young days I remember that, on one occasion when we had been marched to church for confessing, we who were waiting our turn were startled to hear our stolid and venerable confessor audibly exclaim, repeating with horrified accent some statement of his youthful penitent, 'Eighty-three times!' We knew little about the seal in those days, and the boy himself did not grudge us the joke we had against him for many a day.

The penance which is inflicted usually consists of a few prayers. Corporal penances are now practically unknown, and even long and frequently repeated prayer is rarely imposed in England; in Ireland a prayer that will last half an hour, and will have to be repeated daily for months, is often imposed on the luckless Celts. I soon found the utter uselessness of imposing heavy penances from the number of people who accused themselves of having neglected their penance; and those who did not curtail it hurried through it with precipitate haste. For it is customary to kneel and say the penance immediately after the confession, and as there are some score of idle witnesses calculating its severity from the time expended on it, and thence inferring the gravity of the debt, brevity is a feature of some importance. Hence I never imposed more than five or six Pater Nosters. On one occasion I imposed the usual 'Four Hail Marys' on a quiet, unoffending old priest: he was slightly deaf, and, changing his posture of deep humility, he looked up at me indignantly, exclaiming 'Forty Hail Marys!'

Short penances were not the only deviation from our theological rules which I allowed myself: I soon abandoned the hateful practice of interrogating on malodorous subjects. At first when I heard a general accusation I merely asked whether the morbidity in question was serious or not (for if it were not serious there was no obligation to interrogate): I was, however, so indignantly repulsed when the lady did happen to be on the safe side that I was compelled to resort to the usual Socratic dialogue. It was not long, however, before I entirely abandoned the practice, and simply allowed my penitents to say what they thought necessary. Theologians will tell me that on that point alone (if there were no others) I am damned eternally—for I shall certainly never repent of it—but I could not convince myself that such an order ever emanated from the lips of the gentle, woman-loving Christ. However, the Church imposes the obligation under pain of mortal sin, and I do not doubt that some of my perplexed colleagues will see in that sin the reason of the withdrawal of the light of faith from me. In any case the whole institution had become profoundly hateful and repulsive to me, and I eagerly embraced an opportunity to escape from it soon after I had commenced, by a course of study at Louvain University.

CHAPTER VII

A YEAR AT LOUVAIN

LOUVAIN UNIVERSITY is the principal Roman Catholic University in the north of Europe. Nominally it is a centre of higher Catholic instruction for all the northern countries, including, until a recent date, the United States of America. However it is, in point of fact, little more than a national institution. The patriotic Germans naturally prefer their own vigorous, though less venerable, University of Innspruck. Britons and Americans have always been represented in its colleges very sparsely, for they have been usually attracted to the fountain head, to Rome, in their thirst for higher doctrine; now America has its great Washington University, and English Catholicism will, ere long, bring to an end its self-imposed banishment from Oxford and Cambridge. The recent efforts to form a Catholic colony at Cambridge have awakened the Jesuits to a counter demonstration of zeal at Oxford; in any case, the vague opposition of ecclesiastical authorities to the sending of Catholics to our great Universities has for some time been steadily on the wane. Ecclesiastics, of course, will still have to be sent abroad to develop in a purer atmosphere, and will continue to prefer Rome to Louvain; large numbers of them still receive their ordinary training in Spain or at Rome. Still Louvain could boast many nationalities amongst its 1,600 students.

The long struggle between Catholicism and Liberalism in Belgium has had the effect of marking off Louvain amongst its universities as distinctively Catholic. Distinguished by a long tradition of orthodoxy and many illustrious names, the clerical party concentrated themselves upon it, and determined to exclude the liberalising tendencies which had either mastered, or threatened to master, the other universities, Brussels, Ghent, &c. The control is exclusively clerical, both rector and vice-rector being high ecclesiastical dignitaries, and every orthodox family with a care for the orthodox training of its sons is expected to send them to Louvain.

It is a great error to suppose, however, that Louvain is, like the Roman institutions, merely a centre of clerical training; Belgian Catholicism is fallen much too low to realise so ambitious a dream. During the year which I spent there—1893-4—there were not more than fifty clerical students out of the 1,600; ecclesiastical studies were, therefore, working at a dead loss, for the theological staff was numerous and distinguished. The greater part of the students were in law and medicine, though there were also sections for engineering, brewery, and other technical branches. Moreover the university suffered from the presence of a rival clerical establishment in the same town—conducted, of course, by the Jesuits. The Jesuits, the 'Thundering legion' of the ecclesiastical army, have one weakness from a disciplinary point of view—they never co-operate; 'aut Cæsar aut nullus' is their motto whenever they commence operations in a new locality. And so at Louvain, after, it is said, a long and fruitless effort to secure the monopoly of the university itself, they have erected a splendid and efficient college, in which the lectures are thrown open to outsiders, and from which a brilliant student is occasionally sent to throw down his glove to the university, to defend thirty or forty theses against the united phalanx of veteran professors. The Dominicans have also a large international college in the town, and the American bishops a fourth, in which European volunteers for the American missions are trained. The rivalry which results, although it does occasionally overflow the channel of fraternal charity, helps to sustain the ebbing vitality of the Belgian Church, and turns its attention from the rapid growth of Rationalism and Socialism.

One difference between the Belgian and the English system is that few of the students live in the colleges, scattered at intervals over the town, which form the university. They are usually only lecture halls, and their attendant rooms and museums; the students live in the houses of the townspeople, for the town exists merely for the accommodation of the university. The vice-president keeps a record of all houses and the addresses of the students; still any student of Oxford or Cambridge will appreciate the probable value of such a liberty. A second and most important difference from English university life lies in the utter absence of athleticism. The Belgians were entirely averse to muscular exertion of any kind. I saw very little cycling, no cricket, no football, no rowing—nothing more active than skittles during the whole period, for 'beer and skittles' is much more than a figurative ideal to the Belgian. Their free time, and they are not at all a studious race, is mainly spent in the *estaminets* or beer houses, and, like German students, they consume enormous quantities of their national beverage and smoke unceasingly.

The ethical result of such a mode of life may be deduced from general physiological laws. The 'rector magnificus' is a very able and estimable man, but of a retiring and studious character; the vice-rector, Mgr. Cartuyvels, is, however, an active and zealous disciplinarian, and, by means of a wide system of *espionage*, he is tolerably acquainted with the condition of affairs. Still he is powerless to stem an inevitable tide, and indeed it is said that he is afraid to enforce his authority too sternly, lest he should drive more Catholics to the other Liberal universities. Of the two evils, heterodoxy or immorality, the Church naturally prefers the latter, though it is said that the religion of the students is not of much more value than their morality. I was informed by a Louvain priest that at least 500 out of the 1,500 did not attend Mass on Sundays ; and, in the Church of Rome, attendance is obligatory and a test of communion. Like that of so many of our Hibernian neighbours, their faith is only brought to a practical issue in a riot over religious questions. Once the Liberals or the Socialists fill the streets with their anti-clerical cry, ' À bas la calotte,' the students are found to be Catholic to a man, for, as in an Oxford town-and-gown fight, they are vaguely supposed to be sustaining the honour of their ' alma mater ' ; but, apart from such uncanonical, though not infrequent, ebullitions, their piety is of a painfully evanescent character.

The clerical students, who live as a rule in the colleges, are priests who have distinguished themselves in their ordinary theological course, and who have been forwarded by their respective bishops to graduate at the university. Few of them, indeed, reach the full term of a university career and secure the doctor's cap in theology, philosophy, or canon law, for their bishops are compelled by financial and other pressure— frequently by the unsatisfactory results of their examinations—to withdraw them prematurely to the active work of the diocese. The successful student secures his licentiate at the end of the third year, and his bachelorship at the end of the fourth, when he ceases to follow the public lectures at the halls. He then spends two years in the study of his chosen subject, under the tutorial guidance of his late professor, writes a Latin treatise on any thesis he chooses, and finally in the great hall, in presence of a numerous audience, he secures his cap by defending a score of theses against the professors and any ecclesiastic who cares to object. As every religious order, and therefore every school of theology (as was explained in a preceding chapter), is formidably represented in the town, very lively scenes are sometimes witnessed in the discussion of the theses; in fact, certain controversies have had to be practically excluded from the list of debatable questions in order to avoid an undignified delay of the proceedings from the Jesuits and Dominicans in the gallery. The success of the student is, however, practically guaranteed by the mere fact of his presentation by a professor.

The programme of clerical study at the university is practically identical with that of the seminaries, which has been already described: philosophy and theology have the same treatises and the same main problems as in the ordinary course. But they are treated more profoundly at the university: only one treatise is taken each year, and each question is thoroughly exhausted and a large number of subsidiary questions are raised which were crushed out in the briefer elementary course. It is like passing from Huxley's 'Elements of Physiology' to the more exhaustive work of Kirk or Carpenter on the same subject. Then the philosopher has the advantage of attending, with the medical students, scientific courses under men who are eminent in their respective sciences, and the student of theology and Scripture attends lectures in the Oriental languages under equally distinguished professors. In addition to these there are courses of Persian, Sanscrit, Chinese, &c., and courses of the higher literature of most European languages, and of Latin and Greek classics. There is, however, no degree corresponding to the English M.A., and literary studies suffer in consequence. All the clerical students are intended by their bishops to become professors in their seminaries, and, in addition to their degree in theology, they are directed to follow the particular course which will benefit them. Still a spirit of narrow utilitarianism pervades all ranks : the lay students have a definite profession in view and have no superfluous industry to devote to supererogatory studies, the priests think of little else besides their theology or philosophy. There are a few disinterested worshippers at the shrine of philosophy and letters, but their number is comparatively small. The course of Sanscrit and Chinese ascribed to the distinguished student of those (and many other) languages, Mgr. de Harlez, seems to have a mythical existence ; Persian is never demanded, and even Arabic (though the professor is an Arabic scholar of the first rank) is rarely mentioned. Hebrew must be undertaken by aspirants for theological degrees, but Syriac has few devotees.

I was requested by my authorities to follow the course of Hebrew under M. Van Hoonacker. In the old province of Grey Friars in England there had always been a professorship of Hebrew, and a desire was felt in certain quarters to emulate the glory of our ancestors in that respect. Taking advantage of a temporary interruption of my course of philosophy, through a re-distribution of our studies, the offer of a year at Louvain was made to me. Weary with struggles against doubt and with premature ministerial activity, I eagerly accepted and made my way to the monastery of our order at Louvain. To the course of Hebrew agreed upon I merely added a course of Syriac (in virtue of which I fondly hoped to disturb my Anglican brethren over the Peschito version of the New Testament), an elementary course of Biblical criticism, and a higher course of scholastic philosophy; much to the disgust of my colleagues, who thought it an insult to their great university not to spend every hour of my available time in its lecture rooms.

The lectures on Hebrew and on Biblical criticism were both given by the young but very able professor M. Van Hoonacker, an efficient teacher and erudite scholar, who crossed swords (with more courage than success) with the great Kuenen. An abler professor of Hebrew we could not have had, and even in handling the delicate questions raised by the Higher Criticism he displayed much wealth of knowledge, and a generous acquaintance with the writings of his opponents, Wellhausen, Kuenen, &c., and much argumentative power. The subject marked on the programme was an introduction to the canon of Scripture; it was based upon the work of M. Loisy, and ran upon the traditional lines. But he quickly exhausted that subject and hastened to his favourite topic, the discussion, against Wellhausen, of the origin of the Jewish festivals. Of erudition he gave abundant proof and not a little ingenuity in the research and grouping of arguments, but it was obvious that few of the students had any large view of the general issues at stake. All scribbled furiously as the professor spoke (for we had no manual) and endeavoured to gather as much detailed information as would suffice for examination purposes.

In private intercourse I found him extremely kind and courteous, and he frequently spoke to me of the difficulty of his position as professor of Biblical criticism, when the Church left us without any clearly defined doctrine about the nature and extent of inspiration in face of modern rationalism; he did not appreciate the liberty of thought which the Church wisely grants until secular science has reached its high-water mark and it knows what it can decide with security. The Pope's encyclical had not yet appeared, but I know that, as a theologian and an expert, he would not be affected by it in his inner thoughts.

The professor of Syriac (and also, in part, of Scripture) was a man of a very different type. He was a very old professor, Mgr. Lamy, an eminent Syriac scholar, though a poor teacher, and one whose opinions on Biblical questions had been fossilised years ago. Like M. Van Hoonacker, he took the first chapter of Genesis as a subject of translation, and devoted more time to his commentaries on the text than to its Syriac construction. The contrast was instructive: every Monday morning we had the Hebrew professor's advanced and semi-rationalistic commentary, resolving the famous chapter into myths and allegories: the following morning, from the same pulpit, Mgr. Lamy religiously anathematised all we had heard, and gave the literal interpretation of fifty years ago. He was kind and earnest, but his method of teaching was so unfortunate that, after one lecture per week for nine months, we knew little more than the Syriac alphabet. Towards the end he startled us one day by commanding us to prepare for the next lecture a translation of a dozen lines of Syriac *without vowel points*. The incident is illustrative of the average Flemish character. We were three in number in the course, and it was my turn to read at the next lecture. However, my companions, fearful of their own turn, endeavoured to persuade me not to attempt such a preposterous task. By dint of great exertion I copied out the translation of the passage and brought it to lecture on the following Tuesday, when my companion, a Flemish priest, snatched the paper from my hand and tore it in pieces.

The third professor whose lectures I followed, Mgr. Mercier, was a gentleman of refined and sympathetic character and one of the ablest living exponents of Catholic philosophy. To a perfect knowledge of the scholastic philosophy he added a wide acquaintance with physical science (which can be rarely affirmed of the scholastic metaphysician) and a very fair estimate of modern rival schools of philosophy. Instead of wasting time on the absurd controversies of the mediæval schools he made a continuous effort to face the deep metaphysical criticism of the German and the English schools—with what success may be judged from his numerous writings on philosophical questions. During the year I attended, he took 'Criteriology' as his subject; he considered it the most important section of philosophy in these days when, after 2,000 years of faith, the neo-academic cry, 'What is truth?' has revived in such earnest.

Unfortunately the modern sophist finds little earnest and disinterested attention, even in universities: modern students of the great science are widely removed from the restless zeal of Athens or Alexandria or mediæval Paris. Mgr. Mercier is also burdened with an obligation to adhere to the teaching of Thomas of Aquin—the least critical, perhaps, of an age of rampant dogmatism— who is the present favourite at the Papal court. However, Rome keeps a jealous eye on Louvain philosophy since the outbreak of heterodoxy under the famous Ubaghs some thirty years ago. It is still under suspicion of Cartesianism in a mild form: M. Bossu is an ardent Cartesian, and Mgr. Mercier is not untainted, but the circumstance is only a matter of concern to Jesuits and other philosophical rivals.

I had much personal intercourse with Mgr. Mercier, and experienced much kindness from him. Like most of the Walloons, he is more refined and sensitive than the average Fleming. For Belgium is made up of two radically distinct and hostile races: the Southern half is occupied by a French speaking people (with a curious native Walloon language) whose characteristics are entirely French, and the Northern race, the Flemings, is decidedly Teutonic, very hospitable, painfully open and candid, but usually coarse, material, and unsympathetic. The two races are nearly as hostile as the French and Germans whom they respectively resemble (though, I think, neither French nor Germans admit the affinity—the Germans have a supreme contempt for the Flemings). Louvain —Leuven as it is rightly called—is in Flemish territory, and Mgr. Mercier, justly suspecting that I was not at my ease with my Teutonic brethren, offered to establish me in his own house, but my monastic regulations forbade it. Both through him and the other professors I have the kindest recollection of the university, from which, however, I was soon recalled.

A secondary object of my visit to Belgium was the opportunity it afforded of studying monastic life in all the tranquillity and fulness of development which it enjoys in a Catholic country. In England it was impossible to fulfil many of our obligations to the letter. It is a firm decree of a monastic order that the religious costume must never be laid aside: it is still decreed in English law that any person wearing a monastic habit in the public streets shall be imprisoned, and although the law has become a dead letter, experiment has shown the practice to be attended with grave inconveniences. The Franciscan constitutions strictly forbid collective or individual ownership, and even the mere physical contact of money: English law does not recognise the peculiar effects of a vow of poverty, and English railway companies and others are unwilling to accept a *billet* from a religious superior instead of the coin of the realm. But in a Roman Catholic country, at least in Belgium (for in France they are grievously tormented by the law), they have full liberty to translate their evangelical ideas into active life: I had heard that the Belgian province was a perfect model of monastic life, and, as I had vague dreams of helping F. David in his slowly maturing plan to reform our English houses, I desired to study it attentively.

It soon became apparent, however, that perfection, in their opinion, consisted very largely in a purely mechanical and lifeless discipline. Much stress was laid upon their exact observance of the letter of the constitutions, which we English friars conspicuously neglected. In most of the monasteries they arose at midnight for office, observed all the fasts diligently, would not touch a *sou* with a shovel, never laid aside their religious habit, and never interfered in secular business. They felt themselves, therefore, in a sufficiently high position to look down compassionately on our English province, and they were sincerely astonished when the late General of the Order, the shrewd and eminent F. Bernardine, quite failed to appreciate their excellent condition, on the occasion of a visit from Rome. In point of fact the province is infected with the idle, intriguing, and materialistic spirit which monasticism invariably develops when it is not under the constant pressure and supervision of heretics and unbelievers.

Their literal fulfilment of the vow of poverty in these unsympathetic times leads to curious complications. In the primitive innocence of the order (its first twenty years) the vow of poverty implied that all the houses, clothing, &c., that the friars used, remained the property of the donors; that money was on no account to be received for their labours; that all food was to be begged. In the course of time the paternal solicitude of the Pope helped them out of difficulties by declaring that whatever was given to the friars became *his*—the Pope's—property. He also instructed them to appoint a layman as syndic to each of the monasteries, who should undertake (in the Pope's name, not that of the friars—the distinction is one of theological life or death) the financial and legal matters which the letter of the rule forbade the friars to undertake; gradually, too, brothers of the third order, who make no vow of poverty, were introduced into the friaries as servants, and a superior could thus always have a treasurer at hand.

In England the friars never troubled either syndic or lay-brother. The superior of each monastery had his safe and bank account, no priest ever went out with an empty pocket, and the authorities made contracts (from which the Pope's name is wisely excluded) and went to law like every nineteenth century Christian. In Belgium the modified scheme of holy poverty (which would have made Francis of Assisi die a still more premature death) is followed out faithfully. All food is sent in in kind by the surrounding peasantry except, usually, meat and beer, which are bought through the syndic: a lay-brother is constantly wandering about the country begging provisions for the friars, and the response is generous both in quantity and quality. The brown habit is sure to elicit sympathy—especially in the form of liquid, and even the railway officials accept a note from the friary when a ticket is necessary: I have travelled all over

Belgium, visited Waterloo, &c., as comfortably as a tourist, without touching a centime from one end of the year to the other.

Their monasteries, too, bear the visible stamp of their voluntary poverty. Linen is never seen in them, on tables, or beds, or on the persons of the friars; and another point in which they imitate the holy apostle St. James is that they entirely deny themselves the luxury of a bath—for the reason which the pious French nun gave to the English girl who asked why she was not allowed to take a bath at the *pensionnat*: 'Le bon Dieu vous verrait!' Gas is not admitted; and, worst of all, they think it necessary to reproduce in their large monasteries the primitive sanitary arrangements of the neighbouring cottages. Our lavatory, too, was fitted up with archaic severity: a battered zinc trough ran along under a row of carefully assorted taps, into which the water had to be pumped every three minutes. There were no hand-basins, there was no hot water, neither comb nor brush, and only a tub of black soft soap was provided for our ablutions.

The fasts were rigorously observed, though, as it is a wide-spread custom both in France and Belgium not to breakfast before midday, most of the friars suffered little inconvenience. At the same time the feasts were celebrated with a proportionate zeal. On an ordinary feast-day, which occurs once or twice every month, the friars would sit for three hours or more, sipping their wine, talking, chaffing, quarrelling, long after the dinner had disappeared. Extraordinary feasts would be celebrated with the enthusiasm of school-boys: there would be banquets of a most sumptuous character with linen tablecloths, flowers, and myriads of glasses; wine in abundance and of excellent quality; music, instrumental and vocal; dramatic, humorous, and character sketches. In the larger convents, where there are about thirty priests and forty or fifty students, there was plenty of musical talent, and concerts would sometimes be prepared for weeks in advance in honour of a jubilee or similar festival; and every priest had his circle of 'quasels'—pious admirers and penitents of the gentler sex—who undertook the culinary honours of his festival.

The quantity of beer and of Bordeaux which they consume is enormous, yet I saw no excesses in that direction: their capacity, however, is astonishing, and there are few of them who do not kindle at the prospect of an extra pint of beer or of a bottle of red wine. The youngest novices take three pints of beer per day, for they take no tea in the afternoon, and soon learn to look out for every opportunity of an extra pint. Spirits are forbidden, though a few of the elders who have been on the English mission have developed a taste for whisky. They tell a curious story in connection with it in one of their monasteries. An English visitor had smuggled over a bottle for a lay-brother whom he had known in former years

Late in the afternoon the lay-brother and one of his comrades were missing from the religious exercises. After a long search they were at length discovered in one of the workshops in a profound slumber, with the half empty bottle and all the materials of punch on a table beside them.

At Louvain they had been forced to build a special entrance to the monastery for the introduction of their beer, for an unsympathetic Liberal lived opposite the great gate and kept a malicious record of the quantity they consumed. One of the greatest concerns of a superior is his wine-cellar, for he knows well that his chance of re-election is closely connected with it: in fact, on one occasion, when I had asked why a certain young friar seemed to be a popular candidate for the highest position before an election, I was told with a smile that 'his brother was a wine merchant.' Wherever I went in Belgium, to monasteries, nunneries, or private houses, I found that teetotalism was regarded as a disease whose characteristic microbe was indigenous to the British Isles.

The first unfavourable impression I made upon my hosts was by my unintelligible refusal to drink. We arrived at Ghent for dinner, and after dinner (with the usual pint of strong ale) four of us sat down to five or six bottles of good claret: I drew the line at six glasses and at once attracted as much suspicion as a 'water-bibber' of ancient Greece or

Rome. At three o'clock a second pint of strong ale had to be faced, and at seven a third; when wine reappeared after that I violently protested—and never recovered their good opinion. Thirst seems to be a national affliction, for even the peasant women sometimes have drinking matches (of coffee) at their village fairs, and the first or second prize has more than once fallen a victim to her cafeine intemperance. It is interesting to note that few of the friars preserve any mental vigour up to their sixtieth year, and that great numbers fall victims to apoplexy.

There are no congregations attached to the friaries, so that their work differs materially from that of English priests. In fact, their life is the typical monastic life, for, as has been explained, canon law prescribes that monastic houses should only be considered as auxiliaries of the regular clergy. The first result, however, is usually a conflict with the priest in whose parish the monks establish themselves, for they attract his parishioners to their services; and they rarely find much favour with the bishop of the diocese. They hear great numbers of confessions, principally of the surrounding peasantry, and have frequent ceremonies in their churches, but, as there are usually many of them, the work occupies little time. The only work of importance which they do is to preach special sermons and give missions in distant parishes, but even that is little in proportion to their vast numbers. One meets amongst them many earnest and devout men who are never idle for a moment, but the majority lead the most dull and inactive lives.

At Louvain there were nine priests and hardly sufficient work to occupy the time of four. There was one earnest exemplary friar who was constantly and usefully occupied; another, equally earnest but differing in method, would exhaust himself one fortnight and recuperate during the next; the remainder led a life of most unenviable inaction—some, under one pretext or another, did absolutely nothing from one end of the week to the other. They were no students— indeed, most of them were grossly ignorant, and their large library was practically unused. In summer they would lounge in the garden or bask at the windows of their cells until the bell rang out the next signal for some vapid religious exercise; in winter they would crowd round their stove and discuss the daily paper or some point of ritual or casuistry, eager as children for the slightest distraction.

Many of them, indeed, between idleness and eccentricity had developed most extraordinary manias. One of our priests, a venerable old friar whose only sacerdotal duties consisted in blessing babies and giving the peasantry recipes (in the form of prayers) for diseased cattle, had succeeded in getting himself appointed as assistant cook. Another friar devoted his time to the solution of the problem of perpetual motion; another had designed a cycle which was to outrun any in the market—if he could devise a brake capable of stopping it when in motion; another explained to me a system of the universe which he had constructed (from certain texts of Genesis) to the utter and final overthrow of materialism—he had explained it to several professors of science, who had admitted its force in silence, and I found myself in the same predicament. Some took to mending clocks, of which they had a number in their cells, others to painting, others to gardening, others to making collections of little pictures of the Virgin or St. Joseph or of miraculous statues. Few of them spent any large proportion of their time in what even a Catholic would consider the service of humanity.

The little knowledge they possessed was usually confined to liturgy and casuistry. Not being parish priests they had not the advantage of daily visits amongst the laity, which is the only refining influence and almost the only stimulus to education of a celibate clergy; and the little preaching and ministerial work they were entrusted with, lying almost exclusively amongst the poor, did not demand any serious thought or study. There are always a few ripe scholars amongst them—very few at the present time—but the majority profess to base their undisguised aversion for study on the letter and spirit of their constitutions—and not without reason, though they forget that the age to which that rule was adapted has passed away for ever. There is no pressure upon them, yet their ordinary studies are conspicuously barren, and, though the Catholic university opens its halls *gratis* to them, it is with great reluctance that they allow one or two of their students to enter it: to graduate they regard as an unpardonable sin.

Their utter innocence of philosophy led them to take a dangerous interest in my welfare, and gave me a practical idea of the way in which Roger Bacons are victimised. Mgr. Mercier had sent me Paul Janet's 'Causes Finales' to read, and whilst I was doing so one of the elder friars came to glance at the title of my book. He considered it for some moments perplexed, and at length exclaimed: 'Tiens! la cause finale, c'est la mort!' I offered no correction, and he departed to discuss the matter as usual. Then one of the younger friars recollected that he had read somewhere that Paul Janet was 'chef de l'école spiritualiste' in France, and, nobody knowing the difference between spiritism and spiritualism, it was agreed that I was busy in the questionable region of 'spooks.' When Mgr. Mercier went on to lend me the works of Schopenhauer (and they had looked up the name in the encyclopedia) there was a serious question of breaking off my intercourse with him and writing to England of my suspected tendencies. Happily I was in a position to treat them with supreme indifference, for I was neither their subject nor their guest: they were paid (by my Mass fees) for my maintenance— which cost them nothing—and even my books, clothing, bedding, &c., had to be paid for from England. Englishmen, in their eyes, are proverbially proud: I was assured from several reliable sources that I had been credited with an inordinate share of that British virtue.

At present they are making strenuous efforts to reorganise and improve their scheme of study: one or two earnest men are striving against the dead weight of materialism which is oppressing them, and possibly time will bring an improvement, though it can only be by a sacrifice in point of numbers which all are unwilling to make. The two points in which the glory of the fraternity is thought to consist are the maintenance of a perfect formal discipline and the increase of members. The Belgian friars are wrongly endeavouring to secure both points at once. They have built recently a large preparatory college which is always crowded with aspirants; but when I asked one of the Belgian friars, in an unguarded moment, whence the aspirants came, he answered with a shrug of his shoulders: 'On y a ramassé la canaille des rues,' and another explained that their training was deeply vitiated by *espionnage* and by an injudicious system of rewards and punishments. Whatever may be their future—and so long as socialism is kept in check they have every favourable condition—it is quite clear that any serious attempt to purify, to vitalise and spiritualise their fraternity will meet bitter opposition, and will, if successful, considerably reduce their numbers: no large body of men will ever again sincerely adopt an ascetical spirit in their common life. And the Belgian province will be healthier and happier for the remainder of its days if it can rid itself of all its *malades imaginaires*, lazy pietists, crass sensualists, and ambitious office-seekers.

. . . . . .

Belgium is claimed to be a Roman Catholic country, and it may be interesting to discuss the extent and nature of its fidelity to Rome in the light of my inquiries and observations. I had many and intimate opportunities of studying it, and I availed myself of them carefully; not only because I took a speculative interest in the question, but on account of the frequent disparaging references I heard to my own heretical country. Moreover, when I noticed in the list of Peter's-pence offerings that Belgium had collected for his Holiness only 200,000 lire, and England 1,200,000, I felt that there was occasion for careful inquiry.

Politics and religion are so confused in Belgium that the religious status of the country has been revealed roughly at every general election. For many years there has been a fierce struggle between Liberalism and Catholicism, in which the orthodox party has been frequently overpowered; and Liberalism, as is well known, is the anti-clerical, free-thought party. It is, roughly speaking, the *bourgeoisie* of Belgium (with a sprinkling of the higher and of the industrial class) permeated with Voltaireanism and modern rationalism: its motto was Gambetta's 'Le cléricalisme, voilà l'ennemi,' or as a Belgian mob puts it more forcibly 'À bas la calotte!' Not that it was at all a philosophical sect: it was purely active, but accepted the conclusions of the philosophers and the critics as honestly as the orthodox clung to the conclusions of the theologian. In any case it was bitterly opposed to the established religion and the dominion of the clergy on every issue. The aristocracy, for obvious reasons, indolently sided with the Church; the peasantry, on the whole, remained faithful out of brute stolidity and imperviousness to argument.

But during the last few years there has been a profound change in the field as Socialism gained power and character. Not very many years ago a young advocate at the Brussels Catholic conference declared himself a Christian Socialist, and was emphatically suppressed by the clerical and aristocratic members: now, if it were not for Christian Socialism, Rome would soon lose its hold of the peasantry. Socialism, avowedly anti-Christian as it is, has secured the industrial classes and is undoubtedly making progress amongst the peasantry. However, it cannot join forces with waning Liberalism, for it hates the *bourgeoisie*; and it has had the effect of arousing the monarchy and aristocracy to some sense of its danger. Thus the power of the Church remains as yet slightly in the ascendant: it can command little more than half the votes of the country.

So much is clear from election results; but in a country which is fermenting with new ideas mere statistics teach very little of themselves. A new party which is hardly a generation old and which has had a marvellously rapid growth is presumed to have acquired a serious momentum: it consists almost entirely of converts, and the average convert is conscious of his opinions and zealous for them. The adherents to the old party may be still, to a great extent, in their traditional apathy, and only need their minds to be quickened in order to change position. And in Belgium, if we merely listen to the clerical party itself, such would seem to be the state of affairs.

It is much easier to test the real fidelity of nominal adherents of the Church of Rome than of those of any other sect or party in existence: it is the only sect that binds its members under pain of grievous sin to certain positive religious observances. Hence it is possible to gauge the depth and vitality of its influence over its statistical members without entering into the sanctuary of their consciences. And so the fact that one third of the students at the only Catholic university systematically neglect Mass has a profound significance. I once heard a dispute between a Premonstratensian monk, a Walloon, and a Franciscan, who was a Fleming, about the religious merits of their respective races; and to a stranger the choice between them seemed difficult. Confession was taken as a safe test, for annual confession is essential, and its integrity is equally demanded under pain of mortal sin. However the Walloon boasted that you could believe a Walloon in the confessional, but certainly not a Fleming. The Fleming admitted that it was true, but he added : 'You can believe a Walloon *when* you get him, for he only comes to confess twice in his life, at his first communion and at death.' They were both old missionaries, and their points were quite confirmed by the others present.

Moreover I had a more intimate experience of the country, which confirmed my low estimate of its Catholicism. During the Easter vacation I migrated to a small convent in the country, about ten miles south of Brussels. The superior of the convent obtained jurisdiction for me, and I did much service in the chapel of the Comtesse de Meeus, in our own great solid iron church at Argenteuil (well known to Waterloo visitors), and in the parish church at Ohain. We monks were forbidden under pain of suspension to assist the dying or to hear Easter confessions : I soon found that if we did not do so a great many people would manage to do without the sacraments. I assisted three dying persons : one was already unconscious and could only be anointed, and her friends were utterly indifferent about even that ; another, a young man, had to be coaxed into making his confession, but refused point blank to receive communion and extreme unction from his parish priest, and died without them; the third visibly condescended to confess, saying that it was immaterial to him—he would if I wished. Many others came to confess, saying that they would either confess to me or not at all. Everywhere, even amongst professing Catholics, there was a strong anti-clerical feeling, though they made a curious exception in favour of monks.

And when I went down to assist at Ohain for the last day of the Easter confessions I found the little parish in a curious condition, even to my heretical experience. The *curé* smiled when I asked how many he expected for confession, and said that he had not the faintest idea. Theoretically he should have known how many had already made their *Pâques*, and how many parishioners he had: it was a simple sum of subtraction, but he was amused at my simplicity. It appeared that there were some hundreds who might or might not make their *Pâques*: in point of fact we had about a hundred more than the preceding year. He did not seem much concerned about the matter, said it was not an abnormal condition, and that it seemed irremediable. It was curious to note that a Protestant mission which had been founded in the neighbourhood for some time had only succeeded in buying two dilapidated 'converts' after heroic efforts. The Belgians, like the French, are Catholic or nothing.

What I observed was amply confirmed by the information which I sought on the subject. The people were indifferent, and even a large portion of the clergy were apathetic. Great Catholic demonstrations there were in abundance, but little importance can be attached to such manifestations. In the great procession of the Fête-Dieu at Louvain I knew there were hundreds taking part who were mere nominal Catholics; and other extraordinary religious displays, such as the procession of the miraculous statue at Hasselt, were largely supported by the Liberal municipality and hotel keepers from purely material motives. Little can, therefore, be inferred from statistics or from external pageantry. The fidelity of the people must be tested, as in France, by their obedience to the grave obligations of the Church. Under such a test the Catholicism of Belgium is not found to be very deep or substantial: one may confidently predict, although the wisdom of uniting religious and political issues may be called in question, a steady growth of the anti-clerical party.

CHAPTER VIII

MINISTRY IN LONDON

From Louvain I was recalled at the close of the first academical year by a revival of my educational functions at London. A new generation of philosophers had arrived, and I had to resume the task of imprinting the conclusions of scholastic philosophy upon their youthful and unsympathetic minds. The theological studies were also conducted at Forest Gate, and all students had to remain under an 'instructor' until they were promoted to the priesthood. As I held that position during most of the time I remained at Forest Gate I had ample opportunity to study the formation of priests, for the instructor is responsible for the material and spiritual welfare of those under his charge. Of the innumerable complications with superiors, and a certain kind of inferiors, which my zeal (not always, perhaps, blended with prudence) provoked, I forbear to speak; but when the authorities added the task of instructor to the lay brothers or servants my powers of endurance failed. Enough has been said in the preceding chapters about the life of the students, so I pass on to a fuller treatment of the sacerdotal ministry, in which I was now thoroughly immersed.

In a monastic house, even in England, there are always more priests than in a secular presbytery; more, indeed, than are necessary for the administration of the parish which is committed to their care. Many of these priests, however, are travelling missionaries whose work lies almost entirely outside their convent. It is customary in Catholic churches to hold a mission, or series of services somewhat akin to the revival services of the Methodists, every few years; it consists principally of a course of the most violent and imaginative sermons on hell, heaven, eternity, &c., and really has the effect of converting numbers to a sense of their religious duties. Although Cardinal Manning, who, in writing and in action, shows a studied disregard of the monastic orders, endeavoured to form a band of secular or non-monastic missionaries, it is usually conceded that the desired effect can only be satisfactorily attained by monks. Hence every order has a number of religious specially trained for that purpose, of whom two or three are found in every monastery.

Their life differs entirely from that of the ordinary monk; even when they are at home they are exempt from community services, from which the constitutions release them for three days after returning from and three days before starting for a mission. They frequently travel long distances, especially to Ireland, and are sometimes absent from their monastery for months at a time. They are, as has been said, the great bread-winners of the community; they receive from five to ten pounds per week for their services, and bring home large sums in alms and Mass-stipends —if a smaller fee is offered them they never return to that parish. In fact I have known a Franciscan superior (whose rule forbids him to *claim* any fee for his services, or to receive any money whatever) maintain a warm correspondence with a parish priest on the insufficiency of his fee. 'Tempora mutantur nos et mutamur in illis,' would be an appropriate motto for the friars to substitute for their time-honoured 'In sanctitate et doctrina' (which, in its turn, was a usurper; 'Deus meus et omnia' was the motto of the simple Francis of Assisi). However, the missionaries have often very severe labours, and many of them work with untiring industry and devotion; they have service every evening with one heavy sermon, an instruction, and a number of fatiguing ceremonies, and I have known many priests to collapse under the constant strain. The enormous number of confessions they hear adds much to their exertions. At the same time there are numbers of them who much prefer the change and comparative comfort of the life to confinement in their monastery; they lighten their task by preaching the same sermons everywhere, and they usually find the presbytery much more comfortable than home—if they do not, the parish priest will ask in vain for a second mission.

Another form of outside work which is less understood is the practice of giving 'retreats' to monasteries, nunneries, and other religious establishments. A retreat is a period of recollection in which the inmates of a convent suspend all study and secular occupation, and occupy themselves exclusively with religious exercises; it usually lasts from ten to fourteen days, and is an annual event. The day is spent in profound silence and meditation, but there are a number of common ceremonies, and two or three 'meditations'—a kind of familiar sermon or *causerie*—are preached daily. The amiable and polished Jesuits are much in demand for retreats, especially by the equally amiable and polished congregations of teaching nuns, but our friars were entrusted with a large number every year amongst the less aristocratic congregations of nuns. A retreat, after a slight experience, is not at all a disagreeable task, and many even of our professors used to spend their vacation in preaching them. The usual method is to write out a set of meditations (the usual graphic descriptions of the 'last day,' heaven, hell, &c.), though cleverer men, like F. David, or men of sincere fervour like F. Bede, make no preparation. The same set of meditations is, of course, used in different places, and five or six sets suffice for a lifetime; for a priest is often invited several years in succession to the same convent, and if the nuns have been particularly amiable and hospitable he accepts. In such cases he must have a new set of conferences, for nuns have long memories, and will look up maliciously if he drops into a passage of one of his former sermons. Besides receiving the usual five or ten pounds, the priest can always rely upon a warm welcome and tender and graceful hospitality from the good sisters during his residence in their convent; and as the convent is very frequently in a pretty watering-place or other desirable locality, it is not surprising that the work is much appreciated.

Then there are minor functions which bring grist to the conventual mill and afford the friars some diversion from the dreary monotony of home life. The secular clergy take annual holidays, and hire a friar at one pound per Sunday to conduct their services for a few weeks; in fact our friary at Manchester took up the work with such zeal (for its missionaries were not appreciated) that it earned the title of the 'Seraphic Cab-stand.' Special sermons, also, are frequently asked, and chaplaincies are sometimes offered to the friars. A neighbouring convent will always demand their services, and even country families often prefer to bring a friar down every Sunday for a couple of guineas than to have a chaplain haunting the premises all the week.

With so many external attractions of a lucrative and congenial character the friars are sometimes tempted to neglect their own parish, which is, or should be, their principal care. The superior of the monastery is always rector or parish priest,[1] and several of his inferiors act as curates; as a rule there is about one priest to every thousand people, less in older and larger parishes—at Glasgow we had six priests to attend to 16,000 people—and more in growing congregations. The work, however, is usually confined to the week end. On Saturday confessions are heard, for it is necessary to confess before approaching the sacrament, which is usually received on Sunday morning. On Sunday the priest has usually a long and very fatiguing day's work; he must, as a rule, say two Masses, an early one for communicants and a late sung Mass at which also he preaches. On account of the obligation to remain fasting, so stern that not even a drop of water must pass his lips until the end of the last Mass, the work is very exacting, especially to a priest who is single-handed. The section of theology which treats of this peculiar fast is interesting; the careful calculation what fraction of a tea-spoonful of water, or what substances (whether flies, cork, glass, silk, cotton, &c.) break the fast, affords serious pre-occupation to the casuist. In the afternoon there are numerous minor ceremonies,

---

[1] In reality all priests in England are merely missionaries, from the point of view of canon law; the bishops are the only real parish-priests. Beyond the fact that they are thus transferable at the bishop's pleasure, the irregularity does not make much practical difference.

baptisms, catechetical instructions, &c.; and in the evening another long sermon with Vespers and Benediction. Speaking from experience I may say that for one man it is as severe a day's work as can be found in any profession.

Here, however, the monastic clergy have the advantage of numbers. Indeed to the ordinary priest it is not so serious a hardship, seeing that, as will appear subsequently, he has six days to rest in from his one day's labour, but to monks even the Sunday is not very formidable. Of the six friars in our community there were never less than three at home on Sunday, so that the work was fairly distributed; one sang the last Mass, another preached at it, and a third preached in the evening, and the remainder of the work was proportionally divided.

The Sunday activity of the priest is patent, however, and curiosity is more frequently manifested with regard to the manner in which he spends the rest of the week. It may be said in one word that the daily life of a clergyman is much the same in every religious sect; family relations apart, the Catholic priest occupies himself in a manner very similar to his Anglican brother (or whatever degree of kindred they may ultimately decide upon). The friar, of course, is understood to follow out a very different and much more serious 'order of the day,' but here again theory and practice have few points of contact. The rule of the friar, who, in a missionary country like England, is unfortunately compelled to take charge of a parish, is simple and reasonable: he must assist at the community devotions which have been previously described, and the remainder of his time must be divided between study and the discharge of his parochial duties. In the morning from eight to twelve he is supposed to study, from three to seven he must visit his parishioners, from eight to ten he must occupy himself once more with study or prayer.

Such is the edifying theory, but the fact is that the more agreeable task of attending to their parishioners absorbs most of the priests' time. There are few friars who, after they have once entered upon parochial duties, give more than a sporadic and careless attention to study. They say that they do not find any advantage for the better performance of their duties in study, and, since most of their 'duty' resolves itself into visits to the sick and chattering with ladies over afternoon tea, their contention is plausible enough; although there are many cases in which their unfamiliarity with modern literature and its great problems brings them into contempt. I have been asked by wives or sisters in the confessional to visit men who were understood to be wavering in faith; I referred them to their parish priests, and was answered that they had so low an estimate of their parish priests that they refused to discuss with them. And where they do meet a Catholic who shows an interest in and acquaintance with modern literature, they are suspiciously forward in urging the restrictions imposed by the Index. If they are not prepared to prime themselves with current literature—and a not unintelligent colleague of mine once frankly admitted that he could not read even the pellucid essays of Mr. Huxley—they take care that their flock does not outstrip them. Indeed, I once heard a professor of dogmatic theology contend that even the ' Nineteenth Century ' is on the Index, and should be forbidden to Catholics; theoretically he was right, yet so curious is the ' economia ' of the Church that it was reserved for a Catholic writer to procure it, by his contributions, a place in the distinguished gallery of the condemned. At any rate a priest who is not studiously inclined finds ample justification for literary tyranny in the elasticity of the Church's policy.

The manner in which they exercise their usurped responsibility is trying to the patience of the ordinary layman. The priest, especially the friar, has very little acquaintance with fiction, still less with science or philosophy, and very wrong ideas of history ; and, since the majority of condemned books are not ' nominatim ' on the Index, but simply involved in the general censure of, ' against faith or morals,' he has to exercise a judgment of an unusually delicate character. The result is confusion and tyranny. One priest is delighted with ' The Three Musketeers ' and permits Dumas—sweetly oblivious of the fact that Dumas is on the Index ' nominatim.' Ouida is much disputed—even amongst the Jesuits; the pure and high principled works of George Eliot are condemned unheard—she was an Agnostic and lived with Lewes; Marie Corelli is dangerous, anti-sacerdotal, so are Mrs. Grand, Rider Haggard, Thomas Hardy, &c., &c.; indeed, the poor Catholic is perplexed before the list of modern novelists. So it is with science and philosophy; the best English and German exponents are heterodox, and when the priest pays his visit and sees their works lying about, he not infrequently demands that they be destroyed.

And his conversation is rendered insipid and uninviting by the same dearth of knowledge and narrowness of judgment. On Biblical criticism, sociology, and a host of prominent questions, the priest is either painfully dogmatic on points that the educated world has long since ceased to dogmatise about, or else he is just as painfully confused. But even on a number of questions on which the world has formed a decided opinion years ago, he is strangely timid and conservative. Rome itself showed much caution in responding to an inquiry about hypnotic phenomena, and such eminent modern theologians as Lehmkuhl and Ballerini seem convinced that in its more abstruse phenomena it embodies a diabolical influence. Even table-turning, of which Carpenter gave a lucid explanation ages ago, is gravely called in question by the Roman decree and the casuists, and, naturally, by the majority. In fact, the author whom I was directed to use in teaching philosophy, Mgr. E. Grandclaude, a widely popular modern author, gravely attributes the more curious manifestations of somnambulism to the same untiring and ubiquitous agency. In every question the priest is found to be ignorant, antiquated, tyrannical.

Hence it is natural that the conversations with their parishioners which occupy most of their time are of a very desultory character. In the morning the friar rarely visits, except in case of sickness, but he is much visited. In every monastery there is a certain section marked off near the door, usually the hall and a few small parlours, to which ladies are allowed access; in the monastery proper, women (except the queen, who cannot be excluded) are never admitted under any circumstances whatever, even to visit a dying son or brother, under pain of excommunication. In these parlours, which, I hasten to add, are fitted with glass doors, the friars are much occupied in the mornings. The rest of the forenoon is spent reading or preparing sermons in their cells, or chatting together in each other's cells, or in the library, or over the daily paper, all of which is illicit but unavoidable. After dinner and early tea they exchange their brown habits for ordinary clerical attire and proceed to visit their parishioners. They are directed to return to the convent at seven, but it is usually much later when they arrive.

Apart from the care of the sick and dying, and the

occasional necessity of reproving wandering sheep, the duty of 'visiting,' which is almost their only function on the six appointed days of labour, is far from laborious. The parish is divided into districts of which one is committed to the care of each priest, and he is directed to visit each family once in three months. The object is, of course, to strengthen the bond between clergy and laity and to secure individual fidelity to the Church. Naturally, however, what really happens is that a few agreeable families are selected for frequent visits, which differ in no respect from the visits of ordinary unconsecrated people (in fact the priest would hardly be welcome who paraded his profession too much); sometimes they are unusually generous benefactors, sometimes mere families of ordinary social attractiveness. In any case, the poor and the uninteresting are forgotten, the favourites are visited weekly or oftener, and the visits sometimes protracted to two or three hours; much jealousy ensues amongst the favourites (who watch each other's houses just as they watch each other at confession), and counter visits, teas, dinners, parties, &c., have to be accepted. Thus the week is easily and not uncongenially absorbed, and a priest often finds that he is scarcely able to prepare a sermon for the Sunday.

Since most of the visits are paid in the afternoon and on week days, it follows that they are almost exclusively to ladies; one result of which is that our English friars are found to be much less misogynous than their Continental brethren who have no parishes to superintend, and indeed many Protestant husbands forbid the admission of a priest into the house in their absence. Much discretion is, however, shown by the priest in visiting, and an excellent control is exercised over all by a comprehensive system of jealousy; the priests are jealous of each other when they intrude in each other's district or parish, the ladies honoured with a visit are jealous of each other, and a numerous non-Catholic population is jealously surveying the whole. In the Franciscan rule besides the vow of chastity there is a special grave precept commanding the avoidance of suspicious intercourse with women, and it is not uncommon for a superior to publicly denounce an inferior for that fault. Two or three cases happened at Forest Gate, but the accusation clearly sprang from jealousy on the part of the superior. In private, of course, mutual accusation, especially of frequenting by preference the society of young women, was very common; there was certainly much truth in the accusations, though why it should be made a ground of *accusation* is not clear. Another rule may be mentioned in this connection: all letters were to be given open to the superior to be forwarded, and he was supposed to read all letters which he received for his inferiors.

There was also a rule, the only one in our constitutions that imposed a grave moral obligation, forbidding us to take any intoxicating drink within the limits of our own parish. The rule led to curious incidents and many transgressions. One old Belgian friar who was afflicted with chronic thirst and did not find the monastic allowance sufficient, used to take the tram regularly to some hotel just outside the limits of the parish. A dispensation could only be obtained by calling together the elders of the community and asking their collective permission. Like all other rules, it was susceptible of many ingenious interpretations, and, finally, the opinion was started that the whole of the constitutions were invalid.

The mutual intercourse of the friars was limited, in theory, to the hour's recreation after dinner. Wine was only granted by the constitutions about once per month, and whisky was entirely prohibited. In point of fact there were friaries in which whisky was given almost every day, every Saturday and Sunday evening, and sometimes three times per day. At Forest Gate, partly from greater sobriety, partly (and very much) from greater poverty, and partly on account of the presence of students, we only drank three or four times per week; whisky was discountenanced, but one friar found port to injure his tonsils, another complained of liver, another of heart, &c., so that it usually crept back to the table. Smoking also was prohibited in the monastery, but it was not very difficult to obtain a medical recommendation to smoke, and the local superior could always distribute cigars when occasion arose.

The nature of the recreation has been mentioned in a previous chapter. We sat and talked over coffee for half an hour, then discoursed peripatetically in the garden for half an hour. In some monasteries dominoes, bagatelle, &c., were introduced to escape the necessity of conversation; cards were forbidden, and chess was discountenanced (with complete success) on the ambiguous ground that the friars had no cerebral tissue to waste on intellectual games.

The conversation only merits description on account of the curiosity which is evinced with regard to it. Politics had the largest share in it, for all the friars were keen politicians, though they dared not openly manifest any political sympathy; they were all Liberals, but for the sake of argument one or other would attack or defend some point in a desultory fashion for an hour or more. Casuistry, too, gave them much food for discussion; and points of ritual and canon law were often discussed. In some friaries there would be one friar of a higher type who would start questions of living interest, but then the conversation was apt to degenerate into a pedantic and not very accurate monologue. But a vast amount of time was spent, as has frequently been suggested of them, in the most painful puerilities. Their sense of humour seems to have undergone an extraordinary degeneration; the more rational of them frequently express their disgust at the character of their 'recreation.' There are one or two powerful characters who habitually tyrannise over the friaries in which they are found, and even contrive at the elections to keep near them one or two less gifted brethren whom they may bully and banter at will. As they are men of high authority and influence, their victims find it expedient to submit patiently to their constant flight of rudely fashioned shafts for a year or two; in the end they usually find themselves elevated to some position to which their intrinsic merit could hardly have aspired.

For throughout the length and breadth of the Franciscan Order (and every other order) ambition and intrigue of office is the most effectual hindrance to fraternal charity. All officials are elected and frequently changed, so that the little province is as saturated with jealousy and intrigue as an American Republic. Every three years a general election is held at which the General from Rome is supposed to preside. The usual course is for the General (whose real name is 'general servant' of the fraternity, but it is usually preferred in the abbreviated form) to send a deputy to the province which is about to hold its elections. The deputy or visitator visits all the monasteries in succession and affords each friar an opportunity, in private conversation, to submit his personal grievances or his knowledge of general abuses. Of the former, however, the visitator takes little notice, referring them to more immediate superiors, and he is usually quite powerless to correct any general abuse. One of our English friars was deputed to visit the

Irish province on the occasion of its election a few years ago. He did not disguise his intention of making a special effort to check the flow of whisky in that province, which he regarded as the source of all evil in monastic life; his own particular vanity was port. We were not a little surprised on the return of our zealous crusader to find that he had been himself converted to the seductive 'usquebaugh,' and only the too openly manifested delight of his numerous enemies—whom he had persistently denounced at Rome for ten years as 'whisky-drinkers'—prevailed upon him to return safely to port.

When the visitator has completed the circuit of the province he invites the members of the higher council, or definitors, to the monastery where the election is held. The superiors, or guardians, of the various monasteries then send in their resignations, together with a declaration on oath by their priests that they have fulfilled their duty to their community (the paper is sometimes minus a few signatures) and a full account of their financial transactions. The guardians themselves arrive the following day and proceed by a secret ballot to the election of a new provincial and his council of five definitors. The guardians then disperse and the newly-elected council proceeds to appoint new guardians with their subsidiary officers. Everything is conducted with the utmost secrecy, the voting papers being burned and pulverised in presence of the voters, and every friar present being put under oath not to reveal the proceedings. Public prayers are also commanded for weeks in advance, and the election opens with a solemn High Mass to the Holy Spirit: an oath is also taken by the electors that they will choose those whom they consider the most worthy.

Such is the admirable theory of the election: its actual course is usually after this fashion. Before the solemn imploration of the light of the Holy Spirit on the election morning the whole scheme has been practically settled. The province is really an oligarchy, not an elective democracy. A few abler men —and better men some of them—form the Definitorium, and there is a sufficiently clear understanding [1] between them and the guardians to insure that the guardians will re-elect them and they, in their turn, will re-appoint the guardians. There is a slight struggle from one or two young Radicals, and perhaps a new aspirant to a place on the council, but changes rarely

---

[1] The following extracts from a letter written by one monastic superior to another may be instructive:

'... they are trying to *force me* to do what I don't think fair or just to my successor ... but I will not do anything that I deem in principle mean or unjust to my successor. I say mean, for I deem it such when guardians to please their superiors send them gifts which the papal Bulls call *bribes*, and which several Popes strictly forbid. But I absolutely refused until compelled by obedience to do such. Of course I was threatened by the "powers that be," that I would pay for it, &c.: but I told them over and over again, "I fear only God and my conscience."'

Unfortunately there were many who had not the firmness, honesty, and deep religious spirit of the writer of that letter.

occur. The old definitors are practically sure of re-election, and so on the night before the electors arrive they have arranged all appointments under no more spiritual influence than that of a cigar and a glass of whisky.

For the highest position of provincial—a quasi-episcopate—the intrigue runs much deeper. Votes are practically bought by minor appointments and other *bon-bons*, years in advance, and the province is really severed into factions headed by the different candidates. There are, of course, some who revolt from such proceedings—though they are more common in ecclesiastical spheres than in any civil polity in the world—but others use them unscrupulously. I took one to task once for his indulgent treatment of a notoriously unworthy official, and he answered frankly that the man had a vote—and he proceeded to explain how necessary it was for the good of the fraternity, &c., that he himself should take the helm at the next election, however reluctant he felt to do so.

When such facts are considered, in addition to the natural jealousy which arises in connection with preaching, penitents, and the esteem of the laity generally, it will be understood that life in a friary is not one of paradisiacal monotony. Open conflicts are, of course, rare, but the strained relations between rivals and their followers frequently manifest themselves in conversation and conference. In fact the constant suspicion and caution sometimes leads to very unexpected phenomena. Thus, a colleague of mine seemed to me in uncomfortable relations with a large number of friars, and of one of them he told me a strange story. He had entered his cell during the friar's absence and found a revolver, which he abstracted and destroyed: he even added that he kept a secret lock on his own bed-room door at night, for the ordinary lock is open to a superior's master-key, and the friar in question was a superior and a priest of high reputation.

Besides the triennial election, called a chapter, there is a half-chapter every eighteen months in which many changes take place. The friars do not, however, as a rule, appreciate the variety which is thus afforded them, for they soon find attachments in a mission which they are loth to break off. But quite apart from elections a friar is liable to be ordered off to a different monastery at any moment. It is related of the celebrated Duns Scotus that when he received the order to go from Paris to Cologne he happened to be away from the Paris monastery. He at once set off on foot for Cologne without returning even to bid good-bye to his brethren. The modern friar is not so precipitate. His 'obedience,' as the formal order to remove is called, allows three days to reach his destination; so that the friar has ample time to collect his luggage (for in spite of his vow of poverty every friar has a certain amount of personal property), and, perhaps, elicit a testimonial from his pious admirers.

Needless to say, the friar no longer makes his journeys on foot as his pious founder intended. There is a precept in the rule forbidding 'riding' under pain of mortal sin, and, in their honest endeavours to discover its application to more modern means of locomotion, commentators are much at a loss. The horse is still gravely prohibited—to ride, that is to say, for in Belgium we more than once had the pleasure of eating it; the ass and the camel are not to be patronised without necessity; a ship may be entered when the friar has not to pay for his sail; even the railway is a matter of serious doubt, but the majority are of opinion that it may be used when necessary—which is a very convenient solution. In point of fact the friar takes his cab, or bus, or train, without a thought of his rule. He has a holiday of two or three weeks' duration, at least once in three years, and frequent runs to the Forest or Southend or Brighton. He cannot, however, leave the country without special permission from Rome.

The 'obedience' or formal order to travel is also a mark of identity for the friar on arriving at a strange convent. For he is always bound to seek hospitality from his own brethren if they have a convent in the town, and the superior's first care is to demand his obedience, on which his destination is marked. This is enjoined as a precaution against apostates and especially against frauds. For even monastic hospitality has been taken advantage of by impostors. In Belgium some years ago the imposition was attempted on a large scale at one of our friaries. A bishop and his secretary presented themselves for a few days' hospitality, and were received and treated by the friars with the courtesy and attention which befitted their rank. There was nothing unusual in the occurrence, and the friars were always glad to receive so flattering a guest. His lordship said Mass daily with correct episcopal ceremony, and had all the requisite paraphernalia. After a time, however, a suspicion was aroused, and when his lordship had casually mentioned the name of the cardinal who had consecrated him, a telegraphic communication was made with Rome, with the result that the impostors were handed over to the civil authority. At London we had visitors from all parts of the world, and it would be difficult to detect an impostor. I remember one whom we turned out of the monastery after a few weeks' hospitality, and no one knows to this day whether he was a genuine friar or not. He was a Spaniard, an old man with our brown costume in his possession, who represented himself as a lay-brother from our province of Mexico. He hinted that a secret Government commission had brought him to London. He spoke French fluently, and was a most interesting conversationalist, representing that he had at one time been a private secretary of Don Carlos and an active figure in Spanish politics. However, Fra Carpoforo's business in London seemed unduly protracted, and our suspicious superiors politely recommended him an hotel in the city.

Impostors find great difficulty in penetrating into the order as novices in modern times, for there are numerous formalities to comply with. Not only are his baptismal certificate and a letter from his bishop necessary, but inquiries are made as to whether there is any hereditary disease, or insanity, or heresy in his family, whether he is single, legitimate, and a host of other qualifications. In olden times anybody who presented himself was admitted to 'the habit of probation' without inquiry, and it is a well-known fact that women have thus obtained entrance into the monastery and remained in it until their death.

An amusing case of imposture occurred at Forest Gate a few years ago. A young man of very smart appearance presented himself at the monastery and intimated a desire to enter the order as a lay-brother. He had no credentials, but mentioned casually one or two friars in other monasteries 'whose Masses he had served.' He represented himself as a cook, saying that he had been at Charing Cross Hotel and other places. Without a single inquiry he was received into the monastery, where he remained for three weeks, cooking for the brethren and maintaining a very modest and satisfactory demeanour. On the third Sunday, however, he vanished with the whole of the money which had been collected in the church on that day and a quantity of clothing, &c., which he had borrowed.

CHAPTER IX

THE LONDON CLERGY

SINCE it will be recognised that the peculiarities which have been described as existing in the life of the Grey Friars are not the outcome of any individual circumstances, but rather the inevitable result of forcing a mediæval ideal on less responsive modern temperaments and in utterly changed circumstances, it will be expected that all the monastic congregations, at least, will present the same curious features. The rules and constitutions of different orders differ as much as their costumes, and their special and distinctive purposes—for each order is supposed to have a special object to justify its separate foundation—also differ; but the difference is again more theoretical than practical. Through the exigencies of their missionary status in England[1] they have been brought down to one common level of parochial activity; the same curious and half-hearted efforts

---

[1] The Archbishop of Canterbury was more correct than he imagined, from a strictly canonical point of view, when he so happily styled the Church of Rome in England 'The Italian Mission.' See note p. 168.

are made to keep up their ritual and ascetical peculiarities in the privacy of the convent as have been attributed to the Grey Friars. *Ex uno disce omnes.*

It was well known by my colleagues that I was deeply concerned at the unpleasant condition of my environment for many years before my secession. I frequently spoke with one of them on the subject, for he professed to be in entire sympathy with me on that point; he used to deprecate it in even stronger terms than I. However, suspecting that I would be thereby tempted to procure a release from the Franciscan rule and pass to some other order (for which permission could be obtained), he would pass on, in all simplicity, to assure me that every other order—and the secular clergy too—was in a similarly unsatisfactory condition.

And I had every reason to be confirmed in the opinion he gave me. Catholic priests have two weaknesses in common with the gentler sex—vanity and love of scandal: one cannot move much in clerical circles without soon learning the seamy side of different orders and dioceses. The different dioceses of secular clergy are jealous of one another, and the secular clergy is generally opposed to the regular: nine secular priests out of ten hate all monks, and nine priests (of any kind) out of ten hate the Jesuits—in fact, I have met very many priests who quite accept the Protestant Alliance version of Jesuitism. Before laymen, of course, every branch of sacerdotalism is treated as little less than angelic—a priest will sing the praises of a priest he hates (I have heard them do it), but a few years' attentive intercourse with different orders and with the clergy of several dioceses has taught me to regard all priests as—human, very human, but neither more nor less.

For instance there are, as was explained in the second chapter, three distinct branches of the Franciscan Order in England; the three sections were as jealous, hostile, and mutually depreciatory as three rival missionary societies, or the three great branches of Socialism. A few years ago the French colony of friars at Clevedon advertised for cast-off clothing for their youthful aspirants for the order; our authorities immediately wrote to Rome and got their action reproved as derogatory to the dignity of the order—the order, it will be remembered, being a *mendicant one*, indeed *the* mendicant order *par excellence*. The French friars in their turn disturbed the peace of their rivals by securing the patronage of the Duchess of Newcastle and pitching their tent within a few miles of Forest Gate; not even inviting us to the foundation of their church. Another day our friars were exalted at the news that their Capuchin brethren (the bearded Franciscans) had been forced to sell their Dulwich monastery to the Benedictines, and again at the rumour that the Capuchins (amongst whom it was said there had been a general scuffle and dispersion—the dutiful 'Catholic Times' gravely announcing that several of their best men had departed for the American missions) were likely to be starved into selling their principal house at Olton. Both these monastic bodies had the same manner of life as ourselves.

Other prominent orders, such as the Dominicans, Benedictines (who are settling in London since Manning's death), and Carmelites, bear much the same relation to their primitive models. The unconscious tyranny of this heretical land prevents a literal observance of their true *régime*, and once the thin end of the wedge of corruption is in it penetrates very deeply. The modern friars have too much common sense and too much sense of humour to attempt a bodily revival of the thirteenth century with its antiquated asceticism and crude religious realism. In olden times every monastery had quite an armoury of spiked chains, bloody scourges, thigh bracelets, hair shirts, &c. In all my experience I have only seen one such instrument of self-torture; it was a thigh-bracelet, a broad wire chain, each link ending in a sharp inward point. It was dilapidated and rusty (not from the blood of victims but from the want of use), and excited as much interest and humorous comment in the party of monks who were examining it as a Spanish instrument of torture does in the Tower of London on a sober Protestant crowd. St. Aloysius, the great model of the Jesuits, was so modest in his relations with the dangerous sex, that he did not even know his own mother by sight; to shake hands with a woman is condemned by all monastic writers as a very grave action. Most Catholic young ladies are aware that the modern monk—above all, the Jesuit—is not all misogynous.

The Dominicans have several peculiar precepts in their rule which they are much tempted to think lightly of; they are entirely forbidden flesh-meat, and they are always forbidden to talk over dinner. I have had the pleasure of dining at their large house at Haverstock Hill on several festive occasions, and I noticed that they trim the constitution a little by adjourning to the library for dessert and wine—apart from the fact that my estimable neighbour did keep up a *sotto voce* conversation with me throughout dinner. I heard a much bolder feat of another Dominican convent. Their precept directs, I understand, that flesh-meat must not enter the refectory or dining-room; the good friars, however, wearied of the sempiternal fish, but saved their consciences on the days they took meat by *dining in another room*. It reminds one of the *pia fraus* of the Dublin Carmelites. They secured an excellent site for a church, but had to surmount an obstacle raised by a former proprietor. He, it appears, did not wish a church to be erected on the spot, so he stipulated that the land should only be sold to a person or persons agreeing to build a house thereon. That was too feeble a net for a theologian; the Carmelites bought the land, erected a fine church on it, and a house on top of the Church.

I met also a curious illustration of that theological ingenuity a few years ago in a Dominican who was practically selling relics—a grave sin in theology. His *modus operandi* was simple. He was commissioned to gather the sinews of war in England to conduct the process of canonisation of a certain French priest, who had tried to live on grass instead of ordinary diet; he had a large number of patches of black cloth, which were said to be portions of the *soutane* of the holy *Abbé*. He could not *sell* them, but he was prepared to *give* one to every Catholic who gave him ten shillings for the cause. It was pointed out, too, that the relics were so large and numerous that if they were collected all over the world they would make a fair number of *soutanes*—no doubt the original had miraculously grown, as the true Cross did in pre-Rationalistic days, so that it has furnished enough timber to build a ship. Besides, it was stated as a mark of the saint's piety that he always wore an old and ragged *soutane*, whereas the relics were pieces of excellent stuff. All this criticism was passed at the time by priests, for it must not be supposed that the clergy are as credulous as they expect the laity to be; they know that the manufacture of relics is a lucrative ecclesiastical industry.

The Jesuits are the most flourishing body of regulars in England as in every other civilised or uncivilised nation. The reason of their success is not far to seek. St. Ignatius founded his society for the special purpose of educating the young; he was wise in his generation, for it is through their splendid colleges that they draw so many neophytes. His children, however, have advanced in wisdom and adopted another main object, and a very worthy and arduous one, no doubt—the spiritual care of the rich. To a good supply of men and money they add a rigorous discipline, and the elements of success are complete. A famous Roman caricature hits off very happily the characteristic feature of the Jesuits and of three other orders by a play on the words of Peter to Christ. A Franciscan, Dominican, Augustinian, and Jesuit are seated at a table of money; the Franciscan repels it with the words 'Ecce nos reliquimus omnia,' the Dominican imitates him, 'Et secuti sumus te,' the Augustinian strikes an argumentative attitude, asking, 'Quid ergo?' and the happy Jesuit gathers in the spoils, with the rest of the text, 'Erit nobis.'

At the same time they are characterised by a remarkable *esprit de corps* which produces an intense isolated activity. The glory of the society is paramount, and always coupled with the glory of the Church; they never co-operate with other orders, but they freely cut across the lines of, and come into collision with, other ecclesiastical forces. Hence there is a very strong feeling against them amongst the clergy and in higher quarters; indeed, one would be surprised to find how many priests are ready to agree with Macaulay and Zola with regard to them. In considering the accusations that are so commonly made against them one must remember how far the acknowledged principles of Catholic casuistry can be extended. It is true that the maxim: 'The end justifies the means,' is reprobated by all sections of theologians (though it is rather closely paralleled by the acknowledged, 'Bonum est diffusivum sui'), still it is only rejected by a quibble; an act which *remains* intrinsically bad cannot be done for a good purpose, they say, but every theologian admits that the 'end' of an action enters into its moral essence and modifies it, and the act must be a very wicked one which cannot be hallowed by being pressed into the service of the Church Catholic—or of the Society of Jesus.

Such quibbles as Kingsley attributes to them in 'Westward Ho!' are certainly defended by Catholic principles and are daily equalled by Catholic priests [1]; and I should not be at all surprised if a Jesuit were to argue himself into accepting the commission which George Sand attributes to the Jesuit tutor in 'Consuelo.' Many priests would admit that M. Zola's account of their activity, in 'Rome,' is probable enough. I once heard F. Bernard Vaughan, S.J., preach a sermon on the title 'What is a Jesuit?' With his accustomed eloquence he summed up the traditional idea—the historian's idea of a Jesuit, and

[1] See afterwards, p. 235.

in refutation, contented himself with detailing the spiritual exercises through which the Jesuit so frequently passes. Although, aided by F. Vaughan's great theatrical power and by the operatic performances which preceded and followed it, the sermon produced considerable effect, it was in reality merely a trick of rhetoric. No one contends that the Jesuit is violating his conscience in his plots, intrigues, and equivocations; regret is usually felt that he should have been able to bring his moral sense into such an accommodating attitude. Every ecclesiastic claims to be unworldly in ultimate ambition; yet even a pope would think a life-time well spent in diplomatic intrigue for the restoration of his temporal power. All such activity is readily covered by the accepted principles of Catholic casuistry.

Still, whatever may have been the policy of Jesuits in past ages their activity in England at the present day is patent. In London they have no parish— except attached to their little church at Westminster, from which they long to withdraw—but they are continually seeking out the wealthier Catholics in various parishes and endeavouring to attach them to their congregation at Farm Street, or send them to help their struggling missions at Stamford Hill and Wimbledon. They have thus excited much hostility amongst the rest of the clergy, but four centuries of bad treatment from clergy and laity alike have sufficiently inured them, and only made them more self-containing and independent.¹ Apart from such petty intrigues for the advancement of the Society there does not seem to be any deep undercurrent of Jesuit activity in England at the present time; in Rome, of course, every congregation and every individual intrigues religiously in the great struggle for canonical existence—under a pope whose whole soul is immersed in his diplomatic and financial schemes what else could be expected?

Besides the great orders there are innumerable minor congregations of regular or monastic priests represented in London: Oblates of Mary, Oblates of the Sacred Heart,² Oblates of St. Charles, Servites, Barnabites, Vincentians, Fathers of Charity, Marists, Passionists, Redemptorists, &c.; most of them are founded by modern priests who had some particular devotion on the brain and, by influence or money, succeeded in getting permission to found congrega-

¹ From several characteristics a parallel is not infrequently and not unhappily drawn between the Jesuits and the Jews.

² As much ingenuity is now shown in devising names for new congregations, especially of nuns, as is shown by our lady novelists in finding names for their heroines. I went some time ago to a small convent which the Duchess of Newcastle has taken under her maternal wing; noticing something new I asked the young nun who opened the door who they were. She drew a long breath and answered that they were the 'Faithful Companions of the Sacred Heart of the Mother of God Incarnate.' A young friend of mine on taking the veil adopted the name of 'Sister Mary Francis of the Eucharistic Heart of Jesus.' Devotion to the 'Sacred Heart of Jesus' is a recent innovation, founded on a private revelation of this century. It was, of course, based on the erroneous belief that the heart is the organ of love.

o 2

tions embodying their idea. Most of them are too hard pressed in the mere struggle for existence to pay much attention to the particular features and objects of their respective congregations. The Servites, it is said amongst the clergy, nearly perished by spontaneous combustion, something similar to the reported *fracas* of the Capuchins; the Passionists were nearly starved out by the indiscretion of an ignorant foreign administration which insisted on full ascetical rigour; the Fathers of Charity have become very modest and retiring since their founder, the celebrated Rosmini, had forty propositions selected from his works and condemned by the Holy Office. The latest is a new order for the conversion of England—of respectable Anglican England, not of its increasing pagan element: it was founded by F. Jerome Vaughan, who seceded from the Benedictines after the interesting *fracas* which was described by a Catholic pen in the 'Pall Mall Magazine' a few years ago.

Besides the great number of regular clergy—who would be more aptly styled the 'Irregulars,' both for a disciplinary reason, and in view of their canonical relation to the rest of the clerical army—there are the ordinary secular or non-monastic clergy. The seculars are those who live in the world (*sæculum*) and the regulars those who live in convents, by rule (*regula*). The seculars have a similar life to the ordinary non-Catholic clergyman; it has been fully described in the preceding chapter, for it is similar to that of the monastic clergy who undertake parochial duties. On Sunday their work is long and laborious: during the week they visit their parishioners and the more attractive of their neighbours' parishioners (which dangerous practice is called 'poaching,' and is watched accordingly), take tea and supper and play cards with them; visit, dine and wine with each other; picnics, parties, entertainments, meetings, special services (with luncheons), visits to the cardinal (after a polite invitation called a *compareat*), occasional holidays help to fill up the inside of the week. They are forbidden under pain of suspension to enter a theatre, or witness theatrical performances of any kind: under Manning, Corney Grain and even Olympia were not thought to be included, but Cardinal Vaughan has proscribed even those relaxations.

They cordially hate the monastic clergy—who have secured most of the best parishes in the diocese—but do not object to dine with them occasionally: I have heard one, at a dinner (though towards its close) in a monastery, unburden his mind about monks in general and our friars in particular in a way which would have been warmly approved by the Protestant Alliance Association. With nuns they are usually on very good terms: they find pupils and novices for the convent, and in return are invited to the innumerable special services, luncheons, entertainments, distributions of prizes, &c., which are equally gratifying to them and to the sisters.

Their circumstances, naturally, differ very widely in different parishes: as a rule they are not rich. Indeed, I have known a priest to reduce his living expenses to nine shillings per week: I should think there are few who have 150*l.* per annum. However, they live in hopes of better days: the State grant to their schools will mean a material increase in their personal income. They, of course, claim it as a relief to their parishioners, but in point of fact the special collections they make for their schools are insignificant: the deficit must be made up out of the ordinary income of the church, which will not change after a concession to their schools by a benevolent Government (whom they will then help to overthrow on the Irish question).

The cardinal usually assists the poorest missions, in some of which, as at Ongar, there are not a score of Catholics: at least Cardinal Manning did, though Cardinal Vaughan has retracted most of his predecessor's allowances. Indeed, they are more afraid of having money taken from them by Cardinal Vaughan than of the contrary, and they fill up their statistical papers with much ingenuity. Cardinal Manning took little interest in the incomes and expenditures of his clergy, but as soon as Vaughan arrived they all received a detailed form to fill in and return, giving an account of their receipts and expenses. Unfortunately the cardinal made a canonical slip in sending the same paper to the secular clergy and to the monastic: the latter are not responsible to him for their conduct *quâ* monks, but only *quâ* parish priests. They therefore held an indignation meeting and protested, with the result that a new form had to be printed which distinguished between their parochial property and income and their monastic affairs, and only demanded an account of the former. Needless to say the answers were very discreet: the Dominicans, it was said, claimed all their business as private.

On the whole the relation of the secular clergy to their archbishop [1] may be described as one of good-natured tolerance; he was not popular in Salford, and he is not popular in the South—in fact, few bishops (if any) are popular with their clergy. He is kind and familiar, and always leaves a good impression after a visit to a priest: he is always much less inflexible than his predecessor—indeed it is complained that he is too easily influenced—and nobody doubts his earnestness and sincerity. He had the misfortune, however, to step into the shoes of a great man, and he has, perhaps, acted unwisely in en-

---

[1] It may be well to explain that the dignity of cardinal is not necessarily connected with episcopal authority: Cardinal Newman, for instance, was not a bishop. The college of cardinals simply represents the clergy of the Bishop of Rome: thus there are cardinal-priests, cardinal-deacons, and cardinal sub-deacons. Cardinals, as such, have no function or jurisdiction; neither have monsignori.

deavouring to tread in his predecessor's footsteps too closely instead of confining his attention to the administration of the archdiocese. The intense activity which has kept him continually on the move since he entered the diocese and which has so rapidly aged him has had little or no palpable result, and has certainly not deepened the attachment of his clergy. His predecessor remained day after day in his little room at Carlyle Place; the world came to *him* and sought his influence.

Yet with all his activity and the perpetual fluttering of aristocratic wings in his vicinity he cannot give the financial aid to his clergy which his predecessor did. One of his first cares was to change the existing financial arrangements, cutting off many allowances and commanding new contributions. He had a perfect right to do so, but when, after so many economical measures, he confessed in his Trinity Sunday pastoral that he could not reach the income of his predecessor his clergy felt little sympathy. In the same pastoral he preached a panegyric of the aristocracy which gave great offence, and he gave a comparison of the contributions of five West-end churches and five East-end churches, which was not quite accurate, was hardly fair, and certainly impolitic. However, he has made many wise changes in the distribution of the clergy and other long-desired improvements. At Barking and Canning Town, for instance, two very poor Irish localities, Cardinal Manning had left for years two priests who were quite unfitted for the work—they were both estimable, refined, and earnest men, who would have been useful in a very different sphere; Cardinal Vaughan has happily transferred them. When the time comes it will prove no light task to find a worthy successor to Cardinal Vaughan.[1]

With regard to the education of secular priests the same may be said as of regulars; in fact the remarks in the preceding chapter apply to the clergy generally. The classical and mathematical training of the seculars is better than that of the friars; beyond, they are entirely in the same condition. Their philosophical and theological studies have been equally disorderly and precipitate: they have had no serious introduction either to the thought of past ages (beyond the thirteenth century) or to the living thoughts of the *Zeitgeist* in our own days. They read little and know little beyond the interminable Anglican controversy. There is a reaction between them and their people;

---

[1] The Vaughan family is a remarkable one; of the seven brothers six became prominent ecclesiastics. Roger died Archbishop of Sydney; Herbert is cardinal; Bernard, the Jesuit, is the first Catholic preacher in England; Jerome is the founder of a new order; Kenelm is a world-wide missionary; John is a monsignore. It is said that John attempted a smart aphorism on the family; he himself represented *thought*, Bernard *word*, and Herbert *deed*. When Bernard heard it he caustically added, 'and Jerome *omission*.' The allusion is to the Catholic classification of sins—sins of thought, word, deed and omission.

the laity are coerced into literary apathy, and consequently the stimulus to study is absent.

About two years ago the cardinal realised that his priests were not *au courant*, and that they were really unable to bring themselves adequately in touch with modern thought, so he instituted a kind of intellectual committee to sit upon modern questions, and report to the majority. A dozen of the better-informed London priests constituted it, and they met occasionally to discuss, especially social questions and the Biblical question. I remember procuring a large amount of socialistic literature for certain members who wished to study both sides. When the members of this new Areopagus had come to a few decisions, they were to enlighten their less studious or less leisured brethren by a series of small books: the books have not yet appeared. The fact that the proposed writers (to my knowledge) dare not print their true ideas on the above problems at present may not be unconnected with the delay. A Jesuit writer, about the same time, began a series of explanatory and very pedagogical articles on the critical question in the 'Tablet,' but he was soon cut to pieces by other Catholic writers. The Jesuits have also published a series of volumes of scholastic philosophy in English. The student will find in them an acquaintance with science and modern philosophy which is rarely found in the scholastic metaphysician. Unfortunately they are little better than a translation of the discarded Latin manuals, plus a certain amount of modern psychophysics; they follow disused shafts of thought much too frequently to be of any real value. The more important volumes seem to have been entrusted to the less important men; whilst there is much acute criticism on minor topics, the treatment of the more profound problems is very unsatisfactory, such theses as the spirituality of the soul and the existence and infinity of God are merely supported by the old worn-out arguments.

What has been said of the perpetual intrigues of the monastic clergy does not apply so forcibly to the secular priests. Each monastery in London is a small world in itself, containing nearly as many officers as privates; to the secular clergy the number of possible appointments is very slight in proportion to their numbers, and thus the fever of ambition is less universal. There is, of course, a certain amount of intrigue for the wealthier parishes, but few of them have any ambition beyond the desire to settle down as rector of some comfortable respectable congregation; in a witty French book a benevolent parent gives as a supreme counsel to his son who has become priest: '*Arrondissez-vous.*' A few may then aspire to the dignity of dean of their district, or to the title of 'missionary rector,' but the genuine Roman fever only begins within the narrow circle of those who presume to aspire to the title of monsignore, or even of canon of the diocese. The dignity of monsignore is not a very significant one; it may or may not be a reward of merit. Any wealthy priest of good family may receive it as a mere compliment. I know one monsignore who received his purple through a monastic order to whom he had given a few thousand pounds, and another (a very worthy man, but painfully commonplace) who got it for his attentions to a distinguished visitor from Rome.

Even canons, as a rule, are very feeble and harmless conspirators; they are generally old men, who are more conspicuous for quantity than quality of service, but have usually sufficient discretion left to know that they are not expected to aspire any higher. In matters of ordinary administration their long experience is often useful to the bishop, with whom they form the chapter of the diocese, but otherwise they have not a very grave responsibility. The same may be said of the titular bishops or those whose titles are *in partibus infidelium*, what are called 'suffragans'[1] in the Anglican hierarchy. The cardinal (and any important bishop) has a number of advisers quite outside his chapter, experts in canon law, professors of theology, &c., who are generally mutually hostile and contradictory, and from their opinions he finally deduces a course of action.

And there is little excitement or intrigue over the

---

[1] The word has a different meaning amongst Catholics; a suffragan is any bishop under an archbishop. All the bishops of England are *suffragani* to the Cardinal-Archbishop.

election to an unimportant bishopric—such as Northampton or Shrewsbury. In fact, a private income is as effectual a qualification as could be desired where the diocese is poor and small, and needs no special energy to administrate it. When the bishopric of Clifton was vacant a few years ago, it was laughingly whispered in clerical circles that the first condition of the candidate must be the possession of the modest private income of 250*l.* per annum. When an important see falls vacant there is naturally much wire-pulling, both in England and at Rome; for the diocese has not a decisive vote in the election of its bishop. The canons meet and decide upon three names to send to Rome, as *dignissimus, dignior,* and *dignus*; however, the Pope frequently reverses the order of the names, and sometimes (as in Manning's election) entirely disregards their *ternum.*

Thus it is that every conspicuous ecclesiastic, whether he be bishop, priest, or monk (for a monk may be raised to the episcopate without intermediary stages), is a continuous object of jealous observation and intrigue, in view of possible cardinal's hats or bishoprics. The state of things which has excited so much interest in Purcell's 'Life of Manning' is only exceptional in that the Church in England is not likely to have such a number of able men simultaneously again for some time; the jealousy, hostility, meanness, and persecution therein described are familiar to every 'great ecclesiastical statesman,' as

Manning is most aptly called. And it must not be imagined that the picture is at all complete—it is not by any means as darkly shaded as the reality. No Catholic could in conscience tell all that is handed down in clerical circles with regard to the relations of Manning, Newman, Ward, the Jesuits, &c. And although the author has made a generous concession in the cause of historical truth, the public have not had the full benefit of his sincerity. If the book could have been published in its original form, it would have been much more interesting, but after spending two years in purgatorial flames as it did, we must take it *cum grano salis*. Some of my colleagues were intimate with the author's brother, and gave us continual reports of the painful progress of the work. About two years before its appearance we were told it was finished, and some very spicy letters and anecdotes were promised; then there were rumours of war, the defenders of Manning, the supporters of Ward, the Jesuits, and others threatening legal action, and the work is said to have been much 'doctored.' On the whole the impression of those who seemed to be in the secrets was, that Newman had been treated by all parties in a manner that dare not be made public, and that there were documents kept back which would throw much discredit upon all other prominent Catholics of the period.

However undesirable such a state of things may be, it is no more than any disinterested person would expect.

The Church cannot change its character in a day; and its past history, like the history of any priesthood under the sun, is uniformly marred by such weaknesses. The life of Cardinal Pie in France, though written by a Catholic for Catholics, gives the same impression; the relations of the Irish prelates and of the American prelates are quite analogous; Rome, of course, is quite a school of diplomacy and intrigue of no gentle character. Such things are inevitable, and it is a clumsy policy to attempt to conceal them and to support the idea that ecclesiastical dignitaries are only guided by preternatural influences. To paint idealised pictures of its own champions and grotesque caricatures of its adversaries (and then sternly suppress all alien descriptions) is rather an antiquated custom; though it is still found amongst many aboriginal tribes.

The actual condition of Catholicism in London is a matter of anxious discussion, even in clerical circles. As will be explained subsequently, grave doubts are expressed as to whether the Church is making any progress at all in England; and this is especially true of London. Catholic journals are not unlike Egyptian monuments: they write large (and in good round numbers) the conquests of the Church, but they do not see the utility of chronicling its losses. Of converted Anglican ministers they speak in warm terms; of seceding priests they are silent—until some other cause brings them into public notice, when they publish a series of reckless attacks upon them and refuse to insert their explanations. Once or twice, however, notices of meetings have crept in at which the opinion has been maintained by priests that the Church is really losing, instead of making that miraculous progress which the average layman believes. Great numbers of Catholics imagine that as soon as the Church of England is disestablished [1] and thus thrown directly upon the support of the people it will vanish almost immediately. I once heard Bishop Paterson explaining that it was undesirable to work for disestablishment just yet, because we Catholics really had not nearly sufficient accommodation for the vast flood of converts that would ensue; we should be quite disorganised.

In point of fact there should be now about a quarter of a million of Catholics in London. Throughout England the ratio of the Catholic population is about 1 in 20, but it is much higher in Lancashire, much lower in London and other places. In Cardinal Manning's time the figures were vague and disputable. When Cardinal Vaughan came down in a hurricane of zeal a census was made of the archdiocese; but the exact figures only established the truth of the pessimistic theory. It was thought that Catholicism did not really know its strength, and that it would be well to proclaim its formidable statistics

---

[1] A Catholic is bound in conscience to desire—to work for, if possible—the disestablishment of the Anglican Church: then he is equally bound to work for the establishment of his own.

to the world; but when the result of the census was known, it was whispered, indeed, from mouth to mouth, but with a caution that the cardinal did not wish to see it in print. He need not have feared: the Catholic press has too keen a sense of its duty (and of its financial dependence on the clergy) to insert such compromising matter.

I have not seen the exact figures—I do not suppose they ever passed the archbishop's study in writing—but I was informed by several reliable priests that out of the small Catholic population of London between 70,000 and 80,000 never went near a church—had practically abandoned the Church. It has been explained that the positive ceremonial obligations of a Catholic are so grave that their continued neglect puts a man outside the pale of the Church. Most priests can fairly ascertain how many nominal Catholics there are in their district—how many *should be* Catholics by parentage, baptism, education, &c., subtracting from this number the average number of attendance at Mass on Sunday (an obligatory service) he finds the number of renegades. So, also, he can make a minimum calculation from his school children; multiply the number of children by five and you have the population, though in some places many Catholic children attend Board schools.

Uncomfortable as the general statement is, a few facts will show that it is rather *under* than *over* the truth. The priest, as a rule, likes to give as roseate an account as possible of his flock, so that in the aggregate there is probably a great loss in point of accuracy. The London Catholics are devoting a quarter of a million to the erection of a cathedral; here are some collateral facts. In the parish of Canning Town in East London there are about 6,000 nominal Catholics; 5,000 of these never come near the church. I was dining with F. Hazel the day the form to be filled arrived, and saw him write it. We measured the church and found that, filling the doorsteps and arch ledges, it would not contain more than 400: certainly not a thousand, mostly children, came to Mass on Sundays, and Easter confessions were proportionate. A question was asked, How many of your youths (15–21) attend their duties? About 5 per cent. was the answer. The income of the parish was deplorable; the vast territory it embraces is full of poor Irish families who live less religiously and not more virtuously than pagans.

At Barking there are more than 200 children in the schools, and the number is not at all complete, and there are not more than fifty adults who attend church; at Grays there is the same condition. A few years ago a zealous priest, F. Gordon Thompson, determined to start a mission in a neglected part of East London—Bow Common; his aim was necessarily small, he could only hope to take care of the children of nominal Catholics. In the first three streets he visited he found 120 such children, and could go no further; their parents he could not attempt to influence. F. Thompson told me that there were several other localities in East London in precisely the same condition. In fact every parish in East London counts at least hundreds of drifted Catholics. Whilst thousands and thousands of Catholics are thus separating from the Church, principally for want of churches and priests, great numbers of missionaries are being sent from Mill Hill, amidst much flourish of trumpets, to India, Borneo, Uganda, &c., and an enormous sum is being collected for an unnecessary cathedral; and the Church of Rome makes a special profession of caring for the poor. Though the phenomenon is not by any means confined to poor districts, it is more conspicuous in them because ecclesiastics are naturally slow to undertake and prosecute such unremunerative toil.

Hence there is such a considerable leakage, as it is called, in the Church that it is questionable whether their 'converts' quite fill up the vacant place. I have thought for many years, and I have been confirmed in the opinion by many colleagues, that for the last twenty years, at least, the Church of Rome in England has made no progress, but has probably lost in numbers; taking into account, of course, the increase of a generation. That the Church has made a large number of converts it is impossible to deny, and it would be foolish to question the sincerity of large numbers of its converts. At the same time the majority of them are of such a class that the change has no deep religious significance. There are thousands of ordinary people whose only convictions, such as they are, regard certain fundamental points of Christianity, and who are drawn into one or other sect by the merest accident—by contact with a zealous or particularly affable proselytiser, by the influence of relatives, by kindness, taste, and a host of non-religious considerations. In fact it is only too clear (and not unnatural) that many associate with the Church of Rome for purely æsthetic considerations. It is well known that many of the much vaunted converts of Farm Street and of Brompton are simply *décadents* who are attracted by the sensuous character of the services, and who would transfer their devotion to a temple of Aphrodite if one were opened in West London with similar ceremonies.

Matrimonial considerations are also very powerful agents in the cause of the Church. Many Catholic priests and families insist upon 'conversion' before admitting a non-Catholic to matrimonial relation. The only 'convert' I am responsible for was a young lady who was engaged to be married to a Catholic; she drank in my instructions like water, never finding the slightest intellectual difficulty; and a few years afterwards, being jilted by him, she happily returned to Anglicanism with the same facility. One of my colleagues was summoned to attend a Catholic who was seriously ill. The wife met him at the door, and asked him to 'be careful, because her husband was only a marriage-convert.' And even when intermarriage is allowed, the Church exacts several promises from the parties in her favour; the non-Catholic is forced to promise that his partner shall have the free exercise of her religion, and that *all* children shall be Catholics, and the Catholic is quietly compelled to promise to work for the conversion of the other party.

Their schools, also, are a powerful proselytising agency. In boarding-schools kept by nuns, whatever promises may be given to parents, it is regarded as a sacred duty to influence the children as much as possible. And, in spite of the notorious fact that girls educated by nuns are less prepared for the difficulties of life and much more liable to come to grief than other girls, numbers of Protestant girls are annually sent to Catholic schools, largely on the ground of economy. Elementary schools, also, are not only the most effective guardians of their own children, but help to extend Catholic influence. Like the consideration which has been urged previously, it is not one to which they give political prominence, but it is certainly an important item in their esoteric programme.

CHAPTER X

COUNTRY MINISTRY

AFTER four years' experience of the life which has been described in the preceding pages, I was not unwilling to encounter some means of escape. Besides the uncongenial environment in which I found myself, my religious troubles had increased every year, until at length I found myself consciously speculating on the possibility of being ultimately forced to secede. The prospect was, naturally, very painful and alarming, and I was resolved to use every honourable means to avert it. However, in the increasing cares of the ministry I could not secure the necessary time for sustained study. I was relieved from monastic duties on account of my professorship, and also from parochial work: I never visited nor received visitors until the last six months. Still, as preacher, confessor, instructor, and professor, I was continually distracted and failing in health, and I eagerly grasped an opportunity of retiring from London which presented itself.

The authorities of our province had at length decided to take action for the improvement of our studies, and a resolution was passed for the erection of a new college for the preparatory classical studies. Hitherto the preparatory college had been a section of our friary at Manchester, and it has been explained how seriously the studies were hampered by that connection. There was a long and interesting struggle amongst the cabinet ministers of the fraternity on the subject; some (especially the one who was directly responsible for the old college) failing to perceive the necessity for a change, some opposing it simply because (as happens in much higher assemblies) they were on the opposition at the time. At length F. David gained their consent to the erection of a new college, and a second sharp struggle followed over the choice of a locality. Some contended that if it were not in a large town and supported by a large parish, it could not be maintained; some (with visions of an agreeable retreat occasionally from their arduous labours) advocated the seaside; others fought for the country. The latter was finally adopted, and F. David entrusted with discretionary powers to make a commencement.

F. David then deputed the task of finding a site to a friar who had the power of living with marvellous economy when circumstances required it. F. David had a large but vague idea that the college was ultimately to be connected in some undefined fashion with Oxford University: in fact, it had not been opened three months before he had, no doubt unconsciously, produced the impression in many quarters that it was just on the point of incorporation. However, no land could be obtained nearer than Buckingham, and there the friar established himself—buying half a field at about three times its value.

The friar lived in the vicinity during the progress of the building, which was erected principally on borrowed funds, as is usual with Roman Catholic institutions. Knowing that the financial prospects of the college were precarious, the good friar set himself to live with great economy and store up a little against the opening of the establishment. He had an excellent reputation for economy already: he knew all the halfpenny 'buses in London, and patronised shops where a cup of tea could be had for a halfpenny. However, he surpassed himself in Buckingham: he read by the light of a street lamp which shone in at his window (thus saving the cost of oil), had no servant, and achieved the fabulous feat of living on sixpence per day[1] during a long period. Being forced at length to keep a lay-brother he chose a poor little ascetic who, he knew, was only too eager to find a superior who would allow him to starve himself on orthodox principles.

When at length it was deemed expedient to remove the zealous friar to another part of England, he had scraped together the respectable sum of 100*l*., which he left to his successor, who, accordingly, in recording

---

[1] The diet was bread, beer and coffee, and tinned meat. For feast-days he used a special meat which cost a penny per tin more.

his disappearance in the 'Annals' of the new college, added that he deserved great praise for the efficient state in which he left the mission. But the newcomer had quite a different theory of life: he agreed with Francis of Assisi that it was irreverent to make provision for the morrow, and so he philosophically made himself comfortable in the little cottage they had rented and religiously trusted to Providence for the future of the college. The income was also doubled through a kind of chaplaincy to the Comte de Paris which he undertook.

In the meantime the councillors were again at loggerheads over the choice of a rector. F. David had asked me to volunteer for the post, and, for the reasons already given, and from a sincere desire to help in reforming our studies, I did so. Subsequent proceedings, however, disgusted me to such an extent that for a time I refused to take it, and several authorities, knowing that I would now have to work it in face of much intrigue and secret opposition, wished to save me from it. I was finally appointed, and entered upon my duty willingly and with earnest and honest purpose. I had incurred the bitter but secret hostility of those who were ostensibly responsible for my financial success; I knew that the province was almost universally hostile to the new foundation; my parish, of some twelve miles in extent, contained only three poor Catholics; I had eight pupils who paid between them the sum of 80*l.* per annum—most of them paid nothing. I had now entered upon the troubled waters of ecclesiastical intrigue, and I give these details n practical illustration of that interesting topic.

Immediately after my arrival the councillors came to the college for inspection and a two days' conference : they prudently sent me a ten pound note in advance. The conference was an interesting one; only one man, and he in a minor position, knew the cost of the building, the amount of debt upon it and annual interest to be met, and the expected source of its income. The others loudly proclaimed that they were going to demand full explanation, security, &c. &c., and that I should be left in perfect tranquillity over financial issues. For two days the little college resounded with loud but, unfortunately, inarticulate discourse. When the last meeting was over I saw by the smiles of the one and the frowns of the others that nothing had been done. I demanded instructions from the provincial, a worthy but obtuse man who had now, by some curious freak of diplomacy, reached—or rather been pushed into—the highest position. He replied blandly that there were no instructions to give me; the Definitorium very flatteringly gave me *carte blanche*. Was I superior of the monastery, such as it was, as well as rector of the college? Certainly : I was chief professor and rector, superior of the house, instructor of the lay-brothers, parish-priest—everything, and I was free to make any regulations, programme of study, discipline that I wished—even free to adopt or not the 'closure' (excluding ladies). I then asked what was the debt, interest, income, &c. I was told not to trouble myself about them; the interest was undertaken by one of the definitors, who also promised to supply any deficit in my income. I ascertained afterwards that neither he nor the others had any idea of the financial condition of the institution. I warned him that the definitor in question was known to be religiously anxious for my ruin and humiliation (for my spiritual good), and that he and his council could not, in any case, shift their responsibility in that fashion. He smiled, shrugged his shoulders, and departed; and I never saw him again.

Under such auspicious circumstances I opened the College of St. Bernardine in October 1895: if betting had been prevalent in our province—we did bet prayers sometimes—it would have been ten to one against my success. During the five months I remained, I received no help from the friar they had spoken of: at the end of that time he stood in my debt. I had not expected it, for I knew that he had another candidate waiting for the rectorship, and that he had openly expressed his intention of letting me come to grief in the position. However, other superiors very kindly and generously came to my assistance—very often simply out of opposition to him—and the initial difficulties were satisfactorily overcome. At my secession, a few months afterwards, the college prospered and its future was quite without anxiety.

I had one associate in teaching, a young and kindly but not very accomplished priest, so that a curious assortment of classes fell to my lot. I taught Latin Grammar, French, Euclid, Algebra, Physics, and a little Greek. And the difficulty of educating them was increased by my utter ignorance of the term they were to remain under me. I remonstrated with the authorities in vain: they were in utter discord themselves, and left everything to chance—some of them hoping the institution would fail. To enliven still further the monotony of our country life there was a revolt of the two servants or lay-brothers. They were both older than myself, selfish and unsympathetic, impatient of discipline: the authorities refused to remove them.

At the same time the bishop of the diocese was piteously calling my attention to the condition of the district, and putting a new charge on my shoulders. There was evidently more duplicity on this point. I was informed that there was no parish attached to the college; the bishop understood that there was, and had promised me a map of it. It mattered little, for the 'parish' would consist of an enormous extent of territory containing three Catholics known and three or four suspected. The town of Buckingham (containing 3,000 inhabitants) boasts of one Roman

Catholic, who, in his rustic diplomacy, attended early service at the parish church and Mass afterwards at the college. Indeed, the whole diocese of Northampton is of the same character: it is the most extensive in England, and only contains a few thousand Catholics.

At Buckingham, of course, it was expected that we were going to re-kindle the light of the ancient faith without difficulty. My two predecessors had left glowing accounts of the ripeness of the harvest, and it was hoped that a congregation would soon be formed round the struggling college. However, I found that the easy tolerance and even cordiality of the townspeople had quite a different meaning. The presence of the French *soi-disant* Royal Family had done much to remove the unreasonable prejudice against Catholics which is found in many agricultural districts. Stowe House had been the chief support of the little town; when the Orleanist family departed after the death of the count, the town was prepared to receive with open arms any institution that would help to fill the void in its commerce. The college was erected just at that period, and, as its future was understood to be one of rapid and unlimited growth, it was warmly welcomed by the inhabitants, who, no doubt, religiously steeled their hearts at the same time against its assumed proselytising purpose. In fact, I found that one or two men who had been duly chronicled as likely to prove the first and easiest converts were confirmed Agnostics who had keenly enjoyed the simplicity of my predecessors. It was soon felt that I was not of a proselytising disposition—apart from the insecurity of my own position, I am afraid I never sufficiently realised the gravity of the condition of our Anglican neighbours—and the college worked in complete harmony with the clergy and laity of the vicinity.

Of my own diocesan colleagues I hardly made the acquaintance. The nearest priest of my own diocese was at a distance of twelve miles to the south; the next, fourteen miles to the north; and there, as elsewhere, the secular clergy do not fraternise with monks. I was now, however, bound to put in an appearance at the casuistry conferences which are held periodically, as has been explained. A diocese is divided into deaneries, and the rectors are summoned every month to a conference at the dean's residence. A programme is printed for each year in which a 'casus'—an incident for moral diagnosis and prescription—is appointed for each conference: a few questions are added which serve to elicit the principles of casuistry on which the 'case' must be solved. A priest is appointed to read the case, solve it, and answer the questions at each meeting; all are then invited by the dean or president to express their opinions in turn, and, as the 'casus' is usually very complicated, a long discussion generally follows.[1] Nearly every

[1] The 'casus' are always in Latin: the following may serve as a

point in casuistry is disputed, and arguments are abundant in the modern Latin manuals—Lehmkuhl, Ballerini, Palmieri, &c. The final decision rests with the president.

A conference in a populous diocese is a very exciting ceremony: rival schools of theology are represented, young priests are pitted against old ones, and the more ambitious are eager to make an impression. But at Northampton our conference was very tame and uninspiring. Only ten priests could be assembled out of a very wide territory, and they were far from being brilliant theologians. A desultory and not very instructive conversation ensued after the case had been read, and in the middle of it the bell rang for lunch, which seemed, of the two, to be the more important function for which we were convened.

The life of a priest in a country parish is usually very dull and monotonous: in our diocese it was not unlike the life of a foreign missionary, so few Catholics there were in the vast territory. I had one parishioner in the town, a poor ignorant creature

---

specimen:—Titius steals a watch from the person of a cleric in church. This he sells to Caius, and nothing further is heard of him. The priest at length identifies his watch in the possession of Caius and claims it, satisfactorily proving it to be his property. Caius refuses to return the watch until his money is returned, and the thief cannot be traced.

Q. 1. How many kinds of sacrilege are there?
Q. 2. How many sins did Titius commit?
Q. 3. How is the case to be solved?

Such a case would provoke hours of controversy.

whose faith was very closely connected with his works; another at a distance of four miles, who was a very doubtful acquisition to the Church; a third five miles off who patiently submitted to being called a Catholic; and a fourth, or rather an excellent family about eight miles off, who had been effectually scared from us by my predecessors: the three or four mythical Catholic harvestmen and washerwomen whom a diocesan tradition located somewhere within the limits of my twelve mile district I never met in the flesh. Most of the other priests in the diocese had rather more souls to provide for, but rarely sufficient to support themselves. They were poor and could not travel much; they had few parishioners with whom they could have congenial intercourse; they were widely separated from each other and had neither books nor inclination for study. The life of an Anglican clergyman in a small country parish is not enviable, but a priest has the additional disadvantage of no family and usually antipathetic neighbours.

When I had at length infused a certain amount of method into the college and of discipline into my small community, my thoughts reverted to the personal object I had in view in leaving London. Surprise is often expressed that the number of seceders from the Roman Catholic priesthood is not higher. Apart from the fact that few people know the number of seceders, as will appear presently, a slight reflection on two points, which have already received attention, will help to understand the matter. In the first place the philosophical and theological studies of the priest have been stunted, one-sided, and superficial; very few of them have continued the work at a university, and even there the work would again be narrow and superficial. They are plunged into active parochial work immediately after their ordination; they have no stimulus and little continuous time to study—except a little casuistry—on the other hand there is ample opportunity and pressing invitation to dissipate their time and wits in agreeable trivialities. Under such circumstances they feel disposed to regard Wellhausen and Kuenen (or even Sayce and Cheyne), Huxley and Spencer, Taine, Draper, and even Anglican divines, as so many literary hedgehogs. Their scholastic system was plausible enough when the professor urged it upon them, and they give no further thought to the subject. Add to this that most of them are Irish, and the happy buoyant Celtic temperament does not take religious doubt very seriously; no one knows into what depths of study and seas of trouble it may lead. In the educated layman, of course, the temperament is sceptical enough, though it is a careless, light-hearted scepticism, not obtrusive and not very consistent; in the priest the same disposition leads to a natural reluctance to take any steps that may lead to a violent dislocation, and to a habit of deprecating a Quixotic striving after mathematical precision and consistency of thought.

And if it happens that doubts do enter into the minds of the clergy (and in familiar intercourse with them one soon finds that they are not uncommon—I have sometimes heard priests openly express the most cynical scepticism) what time has the ordinary priest to make a sincere and protracted study of his opinions? With all my privileges and opportunities for study it cost me the better part of ten years of constant reading and thought to come to a final and reliable decision. The fact that the actual seceders from the Church are usually men who have had special opportunity and a well-known tendency for study is significant enough; the fact that few emerge from the ordinary ranks of the clergy with convictions firm enough to face the painful struggle of secession should not be surprising. Active external occupation banishes doubt from consciousness; to deliberately resort to it for that purpose would be dishonest; few men would subscribe to the Catholic rule, that doubt must be suppressed at once, yet it is the ordinary fate of the clergyman. I experienced a relief myself during the initial labours for my college, but once my work dropped into some kind of routine, the old questions reappeared, and I determined to answer them, cost what it might.

My doubts were of a philosophical and fundamental character. I had felt that, until the basic truths of religion were firmly assented to, the Anglican controversy had little interest for me, and even the

Biblical question was of secondary importance. Accordingly most of my time from my first introduction to philosophy was spent, directly or indirectly, in the investigation of the problems of the spirituality and immortality of the soul, the existence and nature of God, and the divinity of Christ. I had read all the literature which was of any possible usefulness in forming my judgment, and I had been guided (as far as he could) by a man who is thought most competent for that purpose. I drew up on paper the points round which my doubts centred, and added from memory all the arguments I had met in my long researches. I was not influenced by hostile writers, for I had as yet read very little of them, and had been quite unmoved by them; and I had never discussed the questions with a man of opposite opinions. The sole question was, Is the evidence which I have collected satisfactory or not? During the Christmas vacation I studied it without interruption day and night, and finally I was compelled, with great pain and anxiety, to reject it.

The literature which I had studied during the preceding years was principally Latin and French. I had looked for evidence, naturally, in the vast arsenal of Catholic apologetics, and on these fundamental Christian and theistic propositions no better can be found. No philosophy has ever replaced, or ever will replace, the scholastic philosophy as a natural basis for theology. The philosophy of the Scotch school is only plausible in so far as it is Aristotelic; its characteristic elements are extremely unsatisfactory. Martineau is also unwittingly scholastic in his better passages, and he is too much disposed to that 'extra-rational' proof which appealed to Mr. Romanes in his later years: for my part, I would not take a single serious step in this life on extra-rational proof, and I fail to see why it is a surer guide to the next. Thus I came to attach most importance to the schoolmen and the modern writers who adapt their principles to modern thought. I studied with extreme care St. Thomas, St. Bonaventure, Scotus, Suarez, Vasquez, Pontius, Herinx, and a host of other veterans; also an infinity of smaller modern writers, Tongiorgi, Sanseverino, Lepidi, Pesch, Moigno, Zigliara, Rosmini, Lacordaire, Monsabré, &c.

Amongst English Catholic literature there was little to be read. In my younger days I had been taught to shelter myself under the authority of the great Newman: it was a few years before I found that that was rather a compromising position for a philosopher. There is an old adage in the schools that 'in philosophy an authority is worth just as much as his arguments, and no more.' Newman is the last guide in the world to choose in philosophical matters: the key to his line of thought is found in the inscription (epitaph, one feels tempted to say) of his one philosophical work, 'The Grammar of Assent'—the inscription is a text from St. Ambrose, 'Not by logic hath it pleased God to save His people.' Newman was religiously penetrated with that edifying sentiment, hence it is not surprising to find how faithfully he acts upon it in constructing the existence of God and the divinity of Christ. His one witness to God's existence is conscience (he says in one of his sermons that without it he would be an atheist), and under his ceaseless attentions conscience becomes a faculty which few ordinary human beings will recognise; his treatment of it is anything but scientific, it is highly imaginative and grossly anthropomorphic. The text from St. Ambrose is principally intended as a gauntlet for his rival, Dr. Ward; still it is true that Newman had a profound contempt for metaphysics, and, like most people who much despise it, had no knowledge whatever of that science. It is usually assumed that Newman was a traditionalist,[1] but his poetical and unscientific method seems rather attributable to the effect of a wholesome dread of Kant; not that he shows evidence of intimate acquaintance with Kant's 'Critique,' but he seems to have been vaguely convinced that Kant had undermined all metaphysical research, and his own unrivalled literary power enabled him to make a plausible defence of his opinions without the aid of philosophy. He is obviously no guide for a serious scientific mind.

[1] Traditionalism was an important heresy within the bounds of the Church, which was effectually extinguished. It reprobated entirely the use of reason in supra-sensible matters and advocated authority as the sole guide.

His rival, Dr. Ward, also a prominent figure of the great Oxford movement, is the very antithesis of Newman. Newman used to speak contemptuously of the 'dry bones' of Ward's logic, and evidently considered that his own works clothed them and made them more attractive. Ward was a keen dialectician, a subtle metaphysician, and a vigorous writer; his 'Philosophy of Theism,' a collection of essays, is the best English defence of the scholastic philosophy. Unfortunately he was not a man of ascetical temperament, and did not penetrate deeper than he could help into the regions of abstract thought. J. S. Mill was leading him to the critical points of the system in a famous controversy which closed prematurely by Mill's death.

Dr. Mivart is the most influential living writer on the Roman Catholic side, and the most competent to discuss those great problems, 'ever ancient and ever new,' in the light in which they present themselves to the actual generation. Issuing, as he did, from the Darwinian school, it is but natural to expect from him a breadth of view and a seriousness of treatment which happily differentiate his works from those of the usual clerical apologists. Dr. Mivart, however, is not a metaphysician, hence his psychological criticism of Darwinism contents itself with the enumeration of striking points of difference between animal and human faculties which a deeper analysis glimpses, at least, the possibility of harmonising; and this is the only apologetic argument, repeated and enlarged in his successive works, which may be put to Mr. Mivart's credit as useful and original. On other points, such as the freedom of the will, the evolution of ethics, and the origin of the universe, he is conspicuously feeble; and he has a disposition to waste his strength upon the criticism of accidental phases and features of monism and agnosticism rather than upon their essential destructiveness.

Of the Jesuit writers and their series of volumes on scholastic philosophy sufficient has been already said: they have passed some brilliant criticism upon minor issues and aspects of opposing systems, but have made no serious effort to make their more important theses accessible to the modern mind by substituting some solider demonstration for the aerial structures of the schoolmen. Mr. Lilly belongs to the Platonic, sentimental, or semi-sceptical group of apologists. He also is much tainted with Kantism, and offers no solid satisfaction to minds of a severer cast. Like Plato, Kant, Newman, or Balfour, he seems to think it desirable that humanity should cling to certain opinions, and *therefore* seeks evidence in support of them. Of Cardinal Manning's apologetic efforts little need be said. He was a man of action, not of speculation—certainly not a philosopher. His cast of mind is well illustrated by his words to one who was urging certain scientific statements in conflict with Genesis: without listening to them he blandly replied, like the Anglican bishop whom Mr. Stead consulted about the statements of the higher critics:—' I don't believe them.'

I had now exhausted every possible means of confirming myself in my position, and failed to do so. Apart from the fact that, at that time, it seemed to me that the loss of a belief in immortality made life irremediably insipid, I had fearful practical difficulties to expect if I seceded. I had every prospect of success in my position, or, if I preferred, I could have passed to the ranks of the secular clergy without difficulty. I consulted many friends and strangers, and I was confirmed in my resolution to terminate my sacerdotal career, allowing a few months for possible change of thoughts. As the manner of my secession curiously illustrates certain features of Roman Catholic methods and the general question of secession, I describe it at some length in the following chapter.

CHAPTER XI

SECESSION

The Catholic layman has usually a fixed belief in the absolute integrity of his priesthood. He may entertain a suspicion of avarice or of indolence or worldliness with regard to certain individuals, but in point of faith and morality he is quite convinced of the invulnerability of his pastors. At wide intervals a few may be found who are acquainted with a secession, but the report is usually confined with great care to the locality, and the Catholic press—proof against all the ordinary temptations of the journalist when the honour of the Church is at stake—carefully abstains from disseminating the unwelcome tidings. Thus there are few laymen who know of more than one secession, and who are prepared to admit a serious and conscientious withdrawal from their communion. Indeed, there are few priests who know that there have been more than one or two secessions from their ranks, so carefully are such events concealed whenever it is possible.

The secrecy is, of course, not the effect of accident,

for such incidents are not devoid of public interest, and are matters of very deep concern to the Catholic body. The Roman Church claims such a monopoly of demonstrative evidence that it receives a check when its credentials are rejected by one who is so familiar with them; it is—or would be, if it were frankly admitted—a flat contradiction of their persistent teaching that their claims only need to be studied to be admitted. Hence the ecclesiastical policy is to conceal a secession, if possible, and, when it is made public, to represent it as dishonest and immoral. My own position would not for a moment be admitted to be *bonâ fide*; the gentler of my colleagues seem to think that a 'light' has been taken from me for some inscrutable reason, whilst others have circulated various hypotheses in explanation, such as, pride of judgment, the inebriation of premature honours, &c. But of some of my fellow-seceders I had heard, before I left the Church, the grossest and most calumnious stories circulated; pure and malicious fabrications they were, simply intended to throw dust in the eyes of the laity and to make secession still more painful. The majority of priests, when questioned about a secession by Catholics, will simply shake their heads and mutter the usual phrase: 'Wine and women.'

But in the first instance every effort is made to keep secession secret, even from clerics. I have mentioned a case in the note on page 62 which is, I think, known only to a small number of ecclesiastics:

the dignitary in question had not discharged any public function for some years, hence his disappearance was unnoticed. I elicited the fact with some difficulty, and was earnestly begged not to divulge it further. On another occasion, at Forest Gate, I was asked to accompany a canon who was giving a mission there at the time to a certain address in the district. Noticing an air of secrecy about the visit, and a desire on the part of the good canon that I should remain outside, I entered the house with him, and found that it was occupied by an 'apostate' priest. So much I learned by accident, but neither the canon nor my own colleagues would give me the slightest information about him. I never heard of him before or since, and know nothing of his character: I merely mention the incident as an illustration of the concealment of secessions.

And not only is silence enjoined, but deliberate falsehoods [1] are told with regard to seceders. One of

---

[1] It has been already explained that these are not looked upon as falsehoods by Catholic theologians. The case here given is a more direct deception than usual; generally they are quibbles and equivocations which are covered by their remarkably elastic principles of mental reserve and of the necessity of avoiding scandal. Here is another illustration:—

I was gently informed one day at Forest Gate that one of my students had lodged a serious complaint against me with certain higher superiors. The accusation was entirely erroneous; the student had been deceived by another, and I desired to undeceive him by explaining. I accosted him immediately, and asked him if he had been complaining about me. He not only emphatically denied it, but endeavoured, by his manner, to give me the impression that our superiors at Forest Gate seceded or 'apostatised.' My colleagues deliberately told our parishioners that he had gone on the foreign missions; some of them even specifying, under pressure, the district he was seeking. I was myself kept under that impression for a week, so that I could be relied upon not to spoil the story. I believe that even the cardinal was ignorant of the event, for a year afterwards his brother and one of the canons made a suspicious effort to learn from me the fate of the friar in question, of which they were evidently ignorant.

Hence it is that the fiction of the preternatural integrity of the Catholic clergy is successfully maintained. How many seceders there are it is impossible to say, but they are certainly more numerous than is usually supposed. I am at present acquainted with a dozen, but they are widely separated and frequently unaware of each other's existence, so that there may be a still greater number. Many of them are names which were once in honour in the Church of Rome, and are now equally and more widely honoured in Unitarian pulpits or in other spheres of life: many of them being men of recognised literary or scientific ability.

it was the last thing in the world he would dream of. When I told him of the superior's words, he coolly replied that I had had no right to question him, so he was at liberty to deny it. He was a well educated young man of thirty years, son of an Anglican clergyman, and had been two years previously a man of honour, sincerity, and courage. He had been instructed to act as he did by the priests (hostile to me) with whom he had lodged the accusation.

The number is not, however, large in proportion to the number of English priests. The circumstances of their education, literary restrictions, and subsequent occupation are not of a nature to unsettle their minds very seriously. But a still more serious circumstance is the peculiarly painful nature of a breach with the Church of Rome. A breach with any life-long communion is attended with much pain, which is still more intense in the case of a minister of religion who finds himself impelled to that violent wrench of his affections which conscience occasionally dictates: he has formed definite habits of thought and of life and innumerable attachments whose breaking off is accompanied with a pain akin to the physical pain of dislocation and the wrenching asunder of nerves and fibres. For in the Church of Rome, at least, secession means farewell to the past ——farewell to whatever honour, whatever esteem and affection may have been gained by a life of industry and merit. The decree of the Church goes forth against the 'apostate': he is excommunicated, cursed in this life and the next, and socially ostracised, if not worse. The many, the great crowd of admirers, listen to every idle tale that is hatched against him; the few, whose moral and humane instincts are too deep to be thus perverted, can but offer a distant and stealthy sympathy. He is cast out to recommence life, socially and financially, in middle age: perhaps homeless, friendless, and resourceless. A description of the writer's experience of the ordeal may be interesting and instructive.

When I was forced at length to acknowledge that I had lost all faith in my religious profession, I thought to avail myself of my position as superior to enter into secular life with more facility. I revealed my state of mind to several non-Catholic acquaintances —it would have been fatal to my plans and quite useless to reveal it to a Catholic—and they agreed that I must withdraw, after a short time for reflection: only one man, though he is one of the most prominent public men in London, thought that I should be justified in remaining at my post. I began, therefore, to make inquiries and preparations for a new departure. In the meantime I continued to fulfil my duty to the college conscientiously—as a matter of common honesty and in order to give no ground for subsequent calumny.

For the same reason I resolved to take no money from the institution, though I felt that I should have been justified in doing so to some extent. When the superior of a monastery with which I was connected left its walls, he took 50*l.* with him 'as a temporary loan': that circumstance did not excite any particular discussion, and certainly there was no question of prosecution for theft. Similarly, another friar ran away with about 200*l.* My own case, however, was of quite a different character, and would be treated with a very different policy. The two friars were not genuine seceders from the Church: the second was clearly a case of wanton revolt against a recognised discipline, the first was rather doubtful—he only returned to penance after a fruitless effort to find secular employment. In both cases it was evidently the policy of the fraternity to conceal the misdemeanour from the laity: they remained priests, and for the credit of the Church and the prestige of its clergy their faults must be covered over at all costs. But when a priest really secedes from the Church the opposite policy is naturally followed; for the credit of the Church and the confusion of its enemies the seceder must be placed in as unfavourable a light as possible. I was too well acquainted with esoteric ecclesiastical teaching to be unprepared, so I determined to give them no handle. Studies were conducted with perfect regularity; discipline was so severe that my inferiors chafed under it; my accounts were balanced almost from day to day.

At length, I was urgently entreated by a lady at Forest Gate to let her into my confidence, for it was known that I was in great trouble. She was a clever, well educated person with whom I was particularly intimate, and I told her my intention, exacting strict secrecy, and intimating that a revelation would do me much injury, and that nothing could now detain me. I got an hysterical reply imploring me to remain in the Church, and saying that, in case of refusal, I should hear no more from her; she had been my kindest and most intimate friend in the Church of Rome—she kept her word and handed my letter to my colleagues.

A meeting of our cabinet ministers was at once called at Manchester; the two who were more friendly with me were absent, and the other four entrusted F. David with discretionary power to proceed. I had been to London and met him in the train in the evening; he spoke with apparent cordiality about everything except the object of his visit, which he carefully avoided. We sat for some hours chatting pleasantly—and I was fully aware that at the same time he had the order for my deposition in his pocket. However, I was not deceived; I began my preparations for departure the same evening, and kept up the fiction of perfect serenity.

Next morning he at once proceeded to business. He asked curtly of the condition of the college and of my own personality: in both cases I assured him with equal courtesy and curtness that everything was quite satisfactory. It had been the intention of my friend at London, and probably of my authorities, that F. David should induce me to communicate my difficulties and endeavour to remove them. For many reasons, which would have readily occurred to them under less exciting circumstances, it was not my intention to do so; and, as F. David knew that he had counselled me in those difficulties to the best of his power some years previously, I do not suppose that he expected any such confidence from me. He was the only one who had an intimate knowledge of me, having been my confessor during eight years, and he knew that I had arrived at a serious and final resolution. Without further ceremony he handed me the form of deposition from my position, and an order to retire to the friary at Chilworth, in Surrey. Out of curiosity I asked him why I was deposed, and he replied that he did not know.

The friary to which I was ordered is in a very secluded locality. It is the novitiate of the fraternity, and in it I should be compelled to occupy all my time in formal religious exercises, and should be entirely cut off from the outside world, besides being expected to put my confidence in a superior who was absolutely innocent of philosophy, and who would much rather frizzle an Agnostic at the stake than argue with him. It would have been utterly useless for me to go there, now that my mind was firmly convinced, and I preferred to remain and commence my new career with sympathetic friends. To avoid unpleasantness, however, I said nothing of my intention, and prepared to leave the college about the time of the departure of the train; although, when formally asked if I intended to take the train, I refused to say—it was well known that I would not. Meantime I packed up my books, &c., which I sent down to a friend's house: I also balanced accounts and handed over all loose cash except a small sum which F. David had himself offered me for travelling expenses, and which I subsequently

R

returned. At the last moment I was offered the fraternal kiss of peace: I accepted it from my young assistant, but courteously declined it from F. David. I thus turned my back for ever, as I imagined, on monasticism, and hastened down to meet one or two kind and sympathetic friends.

The following morning I strolled down to my friend's office, and was surprised to find him closeted with a friar; it was one of my rebellious lay-brothers (though he had obtained an interview under a priest's name) who had brought a letter from the college. The letter was to acquaint my friend with the fact that a Mr. McCabe, who had been left in temporary charge of the college, had absconded with a quantity of valuable property belonging thereto; that the said stolen property was understood to be on his premises; and that he was informed, in a friendly way, that the matter was in the hands of the police. As a commentary on the letter, the friar gave my friend a long and interesting critique of my public character and mental capacity, and was ejected with scant ceremony. In the impossibility of seeking immediate legal advice we decided to await developments.

In point of fact, I knew there were a few small books amongst my own, overlooked in the hurry of departure, which did belong to the college: these, of course, we intended to return. But the difficulty did not arise from that circumstance. Although my late colleagues did not communicate with me on the subject—if they had done so the same arrangement would have been made without police intervention—it appears that they claimed everything I had removed, even the clothes I wore, which they expected me to ask of them as an alms. The claim was ostensibly based on my vow of poverty or abdication of the right of property; the fact that the college was just as incapable of ownership as I (on their peculiar theory) was ignored, and the new rector, F. David, claimed them in the name of the college. They were books and instruments which friends had given me on various occasions (every friar accumulates a quantity of such presents, which remain his, for all practical purposes): legally (for canon law is happily not authoritative in England) they were my property, and I had no hesitation in thinking myself morally justified after my conscientious labours, and, especially, since most of the donors were hardly aware of the college's existence.

In the afternoon the police-sergeant appeared and claimed the property which had been 'stolen from St. Bernardine's College.' I believe that his proceedings were entirely incorrect, though I was unfortunately not sure of it at the time. However, we disputed the ownership of the property, and he at once collapsed. Then, in order to avoid litigation, I promised to surrender a large number of books if F. David would come to claim them.

Father David came, again bringing, to the increasing astonishment of the little town, the representative of law and order. The interview was held with my friend, for I was absent, at Father David's request. Afterwards we proceeded to the partition of the books, which was satisfactorily accomplished; the instrument was referred to the donor, who adjudged it to me. The next day, wearied to death and alarmed at the attitude the friars had shown, I returned the small sum of money I had taken for travelling expenses. Thus I narrowly escaped an ignominious position which would have increased a thousand-fold the difficulty of entering upon a new career.

Then came the painful desertion of all my late co-religionists. Even relatives, some to whom I was deeply attached, wrote harsh and bitter letters to me. I could not blame them; they were taught, as a matter of religious duty, to regard a secession in a moral light, not as a change of convictions. The following letter which I received from a friend at Forest Gate will serve to illustrate the marvellous and profound revulsion of feeling which takes place in them; I give it the more readily as it came from a man of mature age and good education, one, in fact, who is in a high educational position, and who, but two weeks previously, had spoken to me in terms of high esteem and affection.

'Dear Father Antony,—I am deeply pained to find you have fled from the harvest field and become a scatterer—of what type remains to be seen. It is not for me to reproach you, Father Antony—the worm of conscience will do that efficiently, God knows—but it is necessary I should answer your last letter at once in order to prove my position and give no countenance to yours. You ask me to suspend judgment on you, which means that I should pass judgment on Father David forthwith and dub him slanderer, at the bidding of one who has obviously betrayed a sacred trust.

'With reference to your Upton sermon it is true I suggested its publication for the benefit of your mission. Unsuspicious of heterodoxy I failed at first to catch its true import, but quiet reflection afterwards revealed it to me as a subtle attack on Christianity itself, through the doctrine of evolution as applied to morals and religion.[1] How in the face of this you can still talk of your "religious opinions" is inexplicable, surely? I can just conceive you as an Agnostic with a shred of honesty remaining—but as any other odd fish—No! However it may be, God save you from the lowest depths of unbelief! We know too well the evolution of the apostate.

'Yet I desire to speak without bitterness [?] and

---

[1] He refers to the sermon mentioned on p. 91; there were *just two lines* in it on the 'evolution of morals and religion,' and they were orthodox. The writer it was who came to thank me for the sermon—a most unusual proceeding—and ask for its publication. He repeated his praise and his request twenty-four hours afterwards. It was a plea for the better education of the clergy, and, although it hit my own colleagues in a tender spot (and on that very account so much gratified the laity) they congratulated me on it without a murmur.

shall think of you in sorrow only. If at any future time you think I can give you one helpful word, write to me, and believe me now to remain in simple truth,

'Yours sincerely.'

The writer of the above is considered to be unusually well informed in philosophical matters, for a Catholic, and had been intimate with me for some time. I had, therefore, thought it possible, though improbable, that he would be able to take my secession in a purely intellectual light. After such perverse misunderstanding, and harsh and insulting language from him, I was constrained to abandon all hope of sympathy from Catholics. However, I quote one more letter; it is from one of my colleagues whom I much respect. Kind and generous at heart, he is unfortunately narrow in intellect, and imbued with the orthodox notion of a seceder; the effect of the system is, therefore, again visible. It is too long to quote *in extenso*, but I give the more relevant passages. He commences by saying of my words (in describing the treatment I had received), 'the perverse and degrading sentiments of Roman Catholics' that they are 'as insulting as they are false'; he then defends Father David about the scandal over the books, on the ground of my vow of poverty, adding that he did not think me consciously unjust, or unmindful of my duty to the college, or hypocritical. Then he continues:

'And now having made my protest, let me say, my dear Father, that you were quite right in thinking that I am your sincere friend and brother. . . . You will *never* find any friends so true as the *old* ones [?] and it is to be regretted that you did not, in the dark hours of doubt and temptation, seek help from those whose prudence and experience might have saved you from wrecking your life by this false step. "Vae soli." You did not have recourse to those whom you were bound to consult, but relied upon yourself; or, if you took counsel, it was rather with unbelievers than with those of the Faith and of the Order.[1]

'You know well that other and greater intellects than yours have examined the same questions more deeply than you can possibly have done, and have come to an opposite conclusion' [the writer is, as usual, sweetly oblivious of the fact that, in this century, the number of authorities *against him* is equally high and brilliant, at least]; 'and this ought to have made you distrust your own judgment, doubt the infallibility of your own lights, and feel there was much you have not been able to see, which if you could see, would lead you the opposite way. I fear that this pride may have contributed to bring about the withdrawal of the light. What may also have

---

[1] The reader is already aware that both these statements are absolutely inaccurate. I never took counsel with an unbeliever, whereas I took counsel with the most competent friar we had for eight years, until his counsel was threadbare.

helped is that bitterness of spirit you have sometimes manifested towards others, which is not according to the dictates of charity. Add to that a want of respect for those in authority, and you have the factors which may have helped to bring this chastisement from God. I do not judge you [?]; you must know your own conscience, but I feel I ought to tell you what appears to me as likely to have been the cause of your misfortune. . . . As it is, I can only pray earnestly to God to give you light and grace to see the truth and submit to it, and to beg our Holy Father not to cast you off. . . . That shall be my constant prayer, and one that I confidently hope will sooner or later be heard.

'Believe me, my dear Father,
'Very sorrowfully but very sincerely
'Yours in Christ.'

Here, at least, a kindly and humane feeling reveals itself, in spite of the writer's effort to adhere to the cruel system of his Church. Like the preceding letter, but much less harshly, it persists in viewing my action in a purely moral light: he cannot entertain the possibility of my being honestly compelled by my studies to secede. One pitiful effect of this is seen in his effort to sum up my faults—and he knew me intimately—my 'pride' of judgment is, I trust, obviously excusable, I was bound to form an opinion; and the fault of disrespect and harshness to authority will be understood in the light of preceding chapters. I confess that I have taken some complacency in my moral character after that summary of my *advocatus diaboli*; but it is pitiful to see that a clever, experienced, and humane priest can entertain the thought that a man will be damned eternally for such trivialities. His whole attitude is a significant effect, as in the preceding case, of their system; and it is only as effects and illustrations of that system that I offer these details of my secession.

It would be useless to describe all the incidents that arose at the separation; they were wearisome and painful repetitions of the same unfortunate spirit. During my clerical days I had attracted some suspicion by defending the possibility of honest secession from the Church, and especially of *bonâ fide* scepticism; it was now my turn to be sacrificed to the system which I had resented. It has been explained that the Church is prepared to go to any length to prevent scandal, and the recognition by the laity of an honourable secession of one of the clergy would be a serious scandal; hence little scruple is shown by priests in discussing the character of a former colleague. In my own case I believe that nothing very offensive has been invented; the favourite hypothesis seems to be that indiscreet flattery and premature honours have unfortunately deranged my intelligence, discipline, of course, requiring the usual excommunication and social ostracism. Those of my acquaintances who cannot convince themselves of my mental derangement have the grim alternative of regarding me as having 'obviously betrayed a sacred trust' (to quote my correspondent), and infallibly excluded from 'the homes of the blest.' Only my own immediate family circle (and not all of those) and one other family, out of a wide circle of friends, still regard me as a rational and honest human being.

Such a violent disruption of the past is the lot of every seceder from Rome. Add to it the practical difficulty of re-commencing life in mature age, and some idea will be formed of one great force that helps to preserve the integrity of the Roman Catholic priesthood.

CHAPTER XII

CRITIQUE OF MONASTICISM

BEFORE proceeding to summarise the information regarding monastic life which is dispersed through the preceding chapters, and to make it the basis of an opinion, it will be well to supplement and enlarge it as much as possible. For, however interesting the facts may be in themselves, they would throw little light on the general question of monasticism if it could be thought that they were merely illustrative of the condition of one particular order, and still less if they were said to be the outcome of the abnormal circumstances in which one small branch of that order chances to find itself. Nothing is more fatal to the solidity of an opinion than the narrowness of its empirical basis; and no fault is more frequently committed by English writers on the Church of Rome than that of hasty and undue generalisation. The Roman Church in England is unimportant; it is neither more nor less than a large and active mission in an 'heretical' land. Hence many writers fail to correct the insularity of their experience, and thus have not a due sense of the real proportions of sects and their institutions on the great world-stage; they likewise fail to make allowance for the peculiar effect of a missionary status. To avoid this fallacy the preceding description of monasticism in England, illustrated copiously from the life of the Grey Friars, needs collateral support from other countries or national 'provinces' of that order.

One other province has been described already at some length. The Belgian province, it must be remembered, is in an entirely different condition from the English province. It labours under no financial difficulties (the seven monasteries of the English friars bear a collective debt of about 50,000*l*.), it has no scarcity of vocations, it suffers not the slightest civic or legislative interference with its manner of life. It may be taken as a typical branch of modern monasticism, and is claimed to be such by its adherents. Yet although it differs considerably in literal fulfilment of the Franciscan rule, in formal discipline and ritual, it will be recognised from the contents of Chapter VII. that it agrees entirely with the English province in the features which are important to the philosophical observer.

A slight allusion has also been made to the condition of the Franciscan Order in Ireland. So unsatisfactory is it, from a monastic point of view, that the Roman authorities for many years were bent on extinguishing it. Ireland, the most Catholic and superstitious country in the civilised world, is the richest possible soil for monasticism; men who lead the lives of the mediæval monks will receive from its peasantry the deep reverence and hospitality of the mediæval world. Yet the Irish province of the Franciscan Order (the monastery at Killarney which I described belongs to the English province) is one of its most perverted and enfeebled branches. During years of persecution the scattered friars naturally discarded every monastic feature of their lives, and no amount of pressure from Rome has succeeded in restoring them in these more indulgent days. The friars individually possess money (thus cutting at the very root of the Franciscan idea), wear boots and stockings, and rarely don their habits, have secular servants, and are guilty of many other condemned practices. In a word, their lives are those of the ordinary Irish clergy; their profession of Assisian asceticism is little more than an empty formality.

Another numerous and flourishing branch of the order is found in Holland. Although it is in an 'heretical' country it has full civic liberty and is generously patronised: hence it has grown into a powerful body. During my sojourn in Belgium I gathered that it fell far short of the high standard of the Flemish province, and the fact seemed to be generally confirmed. But shortly after my return to England I received a curious confirmation of the opinion. We received a small pamphlet, written in Latin (for it was not intended to reach the eyes of the laity), having for its theme the condition of the Dutch Franciscan province. It was signed by a Dutch friar, who declared that he was incarcerated (and had been for some years) by his colleagues because he would not keep silence: he had written the pamphlet in his room of detention and managed to have it conveyed to friends in the outer world. He declared that the province was deeply corrupted: that asceticism was almost unknown, and a gross sensualism pervaded their ranks —even mentioning isolated cases of friars being brought home to the monastery by the undignified aid of police-stretchers, 'theologically drunk.' He further declared that the superiors of the monasteries bribed their provincial to overlook the state of things, and that the province secured tranquillity by sending large sums of money to the Roman authorities for their new international college. The pamphlet was clearly not the composition of an insane person, and none of our friars called its accuracy into question. Again, therefore, we meet the same unfavourable moral and intellectual features, much more accentuated than even in the Irish province.

The other branches of the order I only know by conversation with isolated members. The American provinces, North and South, especially those of the United States, present many similar features to the provinces described. The German provinces seem to be slightly better—a little more industrious and studious, as might be expected—on the whole not differing materially from their Belgian neighbours. France approaches more to the Southern type. On the whole, the Spanish and Italian provinces maintain a more rigorous discipline and are less material than their Northern brethren. Still, one can hardly say they are more spiritual in the religious sense: they are notoriously idle, and full of petty ambition and intrigue with their attendant strife and mutual hostility. I have met friars from all parts of the world, and there is a remarkable identity of features in their polyglot narrative.

Something has been said, too, in the ninth chapter, about other religious orders—enough to found an assumption that all are in an analogous condition. And, indeed, such a presumption needs but little, if any, positive proof: it is hardly likely that Rome would tolerate an unusual corruption of one particular monastic order. In spite of their great diversity of character and aim the same forces are at work in each. In fact, the various monastic congregations have so far lost sight of the special purposes for which they were severally founded, that they differ from the ordinary clergy in little more than dress and community-life and ceremonies. The orders which, like the Franciscan, were founded for the purpose of caring for the poor and embodying voluntary poverty in their own lives, are found to be continually seeking a higher level —vying with each other for the patronage of the rich (wherever they can escape the Jesuits), and always choosing a middle class in preference to a poor congregation. The Dominican order was intended to be an 'Order of Friars Preachers,' but it now has no more claim to that title than the other semi-monastic and semi-secular congregations. Carmelites, Servites, Marists, and Oblates were founded in order to increase the cult of the mother of Christ; Jesuits for the instruction of the young; Passionists to spread devotion to the Passion: in all of them the original object has dropped very much out of sight, and there is a very close resemblance of life and activity. It is said that there has been serious question at Rome of suppressing the majority of them and reducing the number to about four of different types, which would suffice for vocations of all complexions.

. . . . . .

We are now in a position to answer with some degree of justice the often repeated question: What is the ethical significance and the ethical value of modern monasticism? The slightest reflection on the origin of the monastic bodies will make it clear that a high degree of spirituality and a keen faith in the supernatural are necessary in the earnest votary of monasticism. The orders have been founded by men of an abnormally neurotic and fanatical temperament, who were capable of almost any ascetical excesses. Extraordinary actions were their ordinary stimulant, and they devoted themselves with ardour to that ascetical rigour of life which the Christian Church has, from the earliest ages, derived from the teaching of its founder. It seems clear that Christ did (no doubt under earlier Essenian influence) lay great emphasis on the merit of self-denial; though it seems equally clear that He did not contemplate the selfish and cowardly system of eremitical and cenobitic life which commenced in the Thebaid a few centuries after His death, and which is still fully exemplified in the modern Trappists and Carthusians. However that may be, St. Bernard, St. Bruno, St. Francis, St. Dominic, &c., translated literally into their own lives, under the influence of an unusually fervid religious imagination, the principles of Christian ethics, as expounded universally up to the fifteenth century.

In those ages of vicarious virtue and expiation they became centres of a great public interest, and attracted many disciples. Then, in an evil hour, they drew up certain rules of life, which were slightly modified versions of their own extraordinary lives, and bade their followers bind themselves by the most solemn and indissoluble obligation to their observance. Such rules could only be observed by men who possessed their own temperament and imagination, and one needs very little experience of human life to understand their scarcity, and the great error of supposing that any large body of men would observe them with fidelity. In the middle ages the average faith of men was much keener than it is in the nineteenth: the disturbing influence of science, of scientific history,

s

and of critical literature was unknown, and tradition was a paramount authority, so that men were not only chronologically nearer to the great drama of the foundation of Christianity, but accepted the traditional version with unquestioning confidence.

However, even in the middle ages, monasticism was no purer an institution than it is now. Soon after the foundation of the several orders there begins the long history of corruptions, reforms, and schisms inside the order, and of papal and episcopal fulminations and historical impeachments from without. Long before the death of Francis of Assisi his order was deeply corrupted; indeed, his own primitive companions had made him tear up, or had torn up for him, the first version of his rule, and it was only by the intrigue of certain patrons at Rome that he secured the papal assent to his second rule. And scarcely had the supreme command passed, during Francis' lifetime, into the hands of Fr. Elias, than a powerful party of moderates arose, and dissension, intrigue, and schism threw the entire body into a fever of agitation. Elias was a clever and ambitious friar, with a much wider acquaintance with human nature and much less ascetical fervour than Francis; the manner of life which he advocated was, like that of modern monks, much more sensible—his error was, also like that of the moderns, to cling to the original profession. And that struggle of human nature against the unnatural standard of life it had somehow adopted has never ceased. The many branches of the Franciscan Order, Capuchins, Recollects, Reformed, Conventuals, and Observants, mark so many different schisms over the perpetual quarrel; yet, at the present day, they are all once more on a common level. And, apart from this internal evidence, secular history gives abundant proof of the periods of deep degradation into which the orders of monks have periodically fallen; if secular historians are not trusted, a judicious selection of papal decrees and episcopal letters would place the fact beyond controversy.

Hence it is only natural to expect that, in these days of less luminous and tranquil faith and less fervid imagination, the spirit of monasticism will be less potent than ever—the more so as a large section of Christianity has now repudiated the ascetical ideal entirely, and emphatically dissociated it from the teaching of Christ. Protestantism first fell upon monasticism, flail in hand, for its corruption, and nearly extinguished it; then it sought theological justification, and convinced itself that monasticism was unscriptural. Although, it is curious to add, there have been many vain attempts in modern days to reanimate it, the vast majority of non-Catholics persist in regarding monasticism as founded on an exegetical error and humanly unjustifiable; and that conviction, together with the causes that produced it or occasioned its formation, has re-acted on the old Church. That mental attitude which in former ages passed at once and instinctively from deep fervour to great ascetical rigour is rarely found now in educated spheres; and that very fervour and keen faith is rarer still in this age of universal soul-disturbing scepticism. It is an age of compromise; moral heroism (such, at least, as is dependent on theological sanctions) is rare, and, as only moral heroes can faithfully live the ideal monastic life, true monasticism is likewise rare.

Such a presumption is clearly borne out by the description of monastic life in many spheres which has preceded. The idyllic life of the monk, a life of prayer and toil and unworldliness or other-worldliness, does not exist to any great extent outside the pages of Catholic apologists and a few non-Catholic poets. The forms of monasticism remain, but the spirit is almost departed from them; one is forcibly reminded of that passage of Carlyle where he speaks of institutions as fair masks under which, instead of fair faces, one catches a glimpse of shuddering corruption. Not that monasticism, judged apart from its profession, is an object of special moral reprobation; its fault, its title to contempt, lies rather in its continued profession of an ideal from which it has hopelessly fallen, and in its constant effort to hide that discrepancy.

There are, of course, isolated members who are deeply corrupted in monasteries and nunneries, as in every other sphere; and there are, also, many individuals of an unusually high character. But the vast majority of the inmates of monastic institutions may be divided, as is clear from the preceding, into two categories. One is the category of those who are religiously inclined, but whose whole merit consists in the equivocal virtue of having bound themselves to a certain system of religious services, through which they pass mechanically and with much resignation, and which they alleviate by as much harmless pleasure and distraction as they can procure. The other category, and, perhaps, the larger one, consists of those who seem to have exhausted their moral heroism in the taking of the vows; for the rest of their lives (and one of the most remarkable features of monks of all classes is the anxiety they show to prolong their 'earthly exile'—doubtless in a penitential spirit) they chafe under the discipline they have undertaken, modify it and withdraw from it as much as possible, and add to it as much 'worldly' pleasure as circumstances permit. Both categories lead lives of ordinary morality—but only ordinary, so that the garments of the saints sit very incongruously on their shoulders, to the ordinary observer; they seem to appreciate the good things of this life as keenly as ordinary mortals, and shrink from death as naïvely as if death meant annihilation instead of entrance into Paradise.

Thus, on the one hand, certain anti-papal lecturers err in representing monasticism, as a body, as an institution of a particularly dark character; on the other hand, the pious belief of the average Catholic layman that it is an institution of unusual meritoriousness—that convents 'are the lightning conductors averting the divine wrath from great cities,' &c.—is pitifully incorrect. Monasticism, not for the first time in its history, has in spite of its high spiritual profession a luxurious overgrowth of sensuousness; indeed, there are many who contend that the whole spirituality of the Church of Rome, paradoxical though it may seem, is generously blended with sensuousness. 'People are led away by the senses,' said F. B. Vaughan, when asked about the operatic performances of his church and the theatrical aspect of his own work, 'and so we must lead them back by the senses.' In monastic life, however, we find a sensuousness pure and simple, quite distinct from the æsthetic influences that are clothed with a religious dignity.

This is partly due to their inactivity, partly to their vow of celibacy. Of their idleness, which is one of the most uniform features of monastic establishments, enough has been said. Their religious ceremonies do not afford serious occupation of mind; they never undertake manual labour in these days, and they are conspicuously deficient in study; the amount of work they are entrusted with does not give occupation to half their members. Hence results much idleness, and idleness, as Francis of Assisi tells them, is the 'devil's pillow.'

Then there is the absence of contact (*entire* absence in Catholic countries) with the sex which is, by instinct and education, more refined, and exercises a refining influence. In the absence of that influence, whose effect is too notorious to be insisted upon, a natural masculine tendency to coarseness develops freely—unless it receives a check in deep spirituality, which cannot be said to be frequently the case. In point of fact most of the founders of orders seem to have appreciated that influence very sensibly. St. Augustine, of course, in his saintly days, does not, for obvious reasons, but St. Benedict had his Scholastica, St. Francis his Clare, St. Francis de Sales his Jeanne Françoise, and even the grim St. Peter of Alcantara had his Teresa. Their modern disciples have also many 'spiritual' friendships, but the fact is unable to counterbalance the effect of their celibate home-life; their intercourse with women, in the face of their ascetical teaching, is necessarily either very limited or hypocritical.

Thus it is that, wherever there is not deep piety, selfish individualism, which is the root of all that undignified intrigue, meanness, and dissension which has been described, is engendered. Thus it is also that there is a morbid craving for indulgence in food and drink—making a mockery of their long fasts and abstinences: in the midst of a long fast they will celebrate an accidental feast-day most luxuriously, and at the close of the fast have quite a gastronomic

Saturnalia. Nevertheless it must be said that, whilst there is much more drink than is supposed, there is not much drunkenness. Usually, as long as the convent is in good circumstances, there is a constant and liberal supply of drink, but excess is rare; though its isolated occurrence, when it has not become public, is not treated seriously.

And a third effect of this pious exclusion of females is seen in the tone of their conversation; it is too frequently of an unpleasant character—not immoral, rarely suggestive, but very often coarse and malodorous. Tales which the better class of Catholic laymen would not suffer to be told in their presence, which could not be whispered in the presence of ladies, and which are only found in such literature as 'La Terre' and 'L'Assommoir,' are very frequently told in clerical circles—especially monastic.

With regard to the important point of immorality, specifically so called, a direct answer must here be given, as far as the author feels justified in giving one. My experience has been wide, but not of long duration, so that I could not deny an opposite and more damaging statement of experience. Still I am convinced that there has been much exaggeration in this respect. The evidence of the majority of 'escaped' nuns and monks seems unreliable; there is only one —the nun of Kenmare, Miss Cusack—whom I should feel inclined to follow. I knew several priests who were well acquainted (indirectly) with her, and they never questioned her substantial truthfulness; at that time she had not made any statements of this particular character, but I believe she has done so since. In any case, if all their tales were true, it would only prove, what everybody expects, that there are many isolated cases of immorality; to extend the accusation to the whole body is unwarranted. It can only be said that these cases are numerous, and that there is a vast amount of solitary morbidity; and there is nothing either startling or instructive in the statement. I have no doubt it would be less true of the clergy than of an ordinary body of men if their lives were healthier; but as long as they are indiscriminately bound to celibacy, and to a life which is so productive of egotism, sensuousness, and indolence, it is the only possible condition for them.

Hence the same must be said of the vow of chastity of the secular clergy as of the asceticism and celibacy of monks and nuns. In theory it is admirable for the ecclesiastical purpose, and very noble and graceful to contemplate from the standpoint of Christian asceticism; in practice it is a deplorable blunder, and in these days of little faith it leads to much subterfuge and petty hypocrisy. Like monasticism, it would not be accepted by one half the number if it were not for the practice of involving them in irrevocable engagements before they are conscious of its meaning. Like monasticism, it will probably disappear when the Church of Rome rises at length from her conservative lethargy, with the din and roar of a vital battle in her ears.

Finally, an answer is also ready to that other question which is not infrequently heard in these days: What is the relation of the monastic orders to Socialism? Socialising Christians, or Christian Socialists, frequently hold up the monastic orders as embodiments of a true social spirit. The argument rests, of course, on a very superficial analogy; there is really no parallel between monasticism and Socialism. On the contrary, they are at the very opposite poles of economics. Monasticism, in the first place (except the modified monasticism of the Jesuits), does not counsel a community of goods; neither in individual nor in common does it permit ownership. But it parts company with Socialism very emphatically when it goes on to impose extraordinary limits on production; Socialism urges a common use of the conveniences produced, and urges the production of as many as possible. And lest it should seem that monasticism at least sympathises with the Socialists of simpler life, such as Mr. E. Carpenter, it must be remembered that it limits production on an exactly opposite principle. Mr. Carpenter thinks simplicity (and sandals) conducive to comfort and happiness; monasticism trusts that they are productive of discomfort and mortification. In fine, it wishes its votaries to be *uncomfortable* in this world, which is the very antithesis of the socialistic aim.

In a minor degree its celibacy is anti-socialistic; whatever relation of the sexes the Socialist may advocate, he certainly advocates some form of intimate relation. And the Socialist would not for a moment sanction the withdrawal of a large number of citizens from every civic duty on the plea that they were more interested in another world. He would not exempt a large number of able-bodied men from labour on the plea that they were 'waterspouts of divine grace' or 'lightning conductors of divine wrath' for their sinful brethren. He would be impatient of all indolence, and mendicancy, and parasitism of any complexion.

However, the parallel has never been very seriously entertained, and does not merit further criticism. Monasticism has neither interest nor advantage for the modern world; it is an enfeebled and corrupted survival of an institution whose congenial environment seems to have disappeared. Even in the stern monasteries of Trappists and Carthusians, where it still retains its full rigour of asceticism and solitude, it alienates the sympathy of the modern world; merit is now thought to consist in the fulfilment of the *whole* duty of man, in works that produce visible fruit, and that tend to remove the actual evils of life. But, for the majority of the monastic bodies, with their indolent withdrawal from life's difficulties and duties, without any real compensating virtue, or with their pitiful compromise between external occupation and their antiquated theories of detachment, one cannot but feel contempt. At the best, a monk would merely have the equivocal merit of making himself a part of a great penitential machine; as it is, his profession of preternatural virtue and unworldliness is a hollow formality that only appeals to credulous devotees.

CHAPTER XIII

THE CHURCH OF ROME

THERE is, at the present time, a profound struggle in progress over fundamental religious questions. During three centuries Europe has resounded with the din, and even been watered with the blood, of conflicting sects; at length other and deeper notes have been struck, and we now find the great sections of Christendom eager to unite under a common banner against a common foe—anti-sacerdotalism, if not a yet more revolutionary force which has been called naturalism. If literature is a faithful mirror of the thoughts and tendencies of its age, no one who is at all familiar with modern literature can ignore that struggle, or affect an attitude of indifference to it. During this and the preceding century the number of most powerful writers and thinkers—from Hume to Huxley, from Voltaire to Renan, from Kant to Wellhausen—who have withstood traditional authority in England, France, and Germany is deeply significant. In our own days, though there is a comparative lull in the storm of controversy and a comparative dearth of eminent thinkers on both sides, the struggle is still conspicuous in every page of every branch of literature. A great number of influential writers are well-known champions of one or other form of naturalism; it is hardly too much to say that the greater number of eminent exponents of literature, science, and art depart in some measure from the orthodox path. It is usually said that women are the more reliable support of clericalism: we have at the present day in England an unusual number of brilliant women writers, but, though few of them (for reasons which may be left to the psycho-physiologist) profess extreme naturalism, few of them adhere strictly to the orthodox sacerdotal institutions. The issue of the struggle is, therefore, the object of much anxious speculation.

The place which the Church of Rome is destined to occupy in this struggle is a matter of much interest, and it is usually conceded that it will be a very prominent position. The Church itself, of course, with that buoyant confidence which is one of the undeniable symptoms of its 'perennial youth,' predicts the ultimate absorption of all other forms of Christianity into itself, and proclaims that the final conflict will be between Rome and Rationalism. And Roman Catholics boast, with much truth, that their prediction is confirmed by many independent observers; Macaulay's vision of the undying glory of the Papacy rising through the mists of future ages over the ruins of England (and, presumably, Anglicanism) finds many sympathisers.

But it is not usually noticed that there is a vast difference in the basis of the prediction in the two cases. Rome prides herself on the intellectual value of her credentials, and thinks that time is sure to bring about their universal acceptance. On the other hand, those non-Catholic writers who talk of an ultimate struggle between Rome and Rationalism are under the impression that Rome does not appeal to the intellect at all: they divide mankind into two categories—rational and extra-rational—and think that the ultimate trial of strength will be between reason and authority, which they identify with Rome. There is a curious misunderstanding on both sides; Roman theologians perversely represent Rationalists as men who reject mysteries, miracles, &c., on the mere ground that they are supra-rational, and without reference to their credentials; whereas many Rationalists are under the impression that the Church of Rome professes an *irrational* method, rebukes and demands the blind submission of reason, instead of offering it satisfactory evidence, and preaches authority from first to last. Under that impression it is not surprising that the Church of Rome is singled out as the 'fittest to survive' of the Christian sects; but the impression is erroneous.

Just as the Rationalist does not reject *supra*-rational theorems if they are not *contra*-rational, and if there is satisfactory evidence in their favour, so neither does the theologian reject the demands of reason for logical satisfaction. The Catholic scheme claims to be pre-eminently logical, and does precisely appeal to the intellect of the inquirer: indeed, it is taught that the 'convert' from Rationalism must have a natural rational certitude, more than what is called a moral certitude, before he can receive the 'light of faith.' The system has been described in an earlier chapter, but the process would be of this character. The inquirer (if beginning from scepticism) would be offered rational evidence of the existence and personality of God, and (usually, though not necessarily) of the immortality of the soul; if that evidence did not satisfy him there would be no further progress. If convinced on those points he would be offered evidence, still of a purely rational character, of the divinity of Christ and Christianity, and of the authenticity of the Scriptures. Then he would be led, on historical grounds, to accept the divine institution of the Church of Rome, its infallible *magisterium* and its indispensable *ministerium*, and the prerogatives of its supreme pastor. He is now prepared to accept statements, logically, on authority, and the rest of the dogmas are, consequently, proved from Scripture, tradition, and the authority of the Church.

But even here reason is not abandoned: not only is it continually sought to confirm statements by rational and historical analogies, but it is admitted as a principle that every dogma must stand the negative test of reason. If any dogma contains a single proposition which offends against reason the whole system must be rejected. Hence much ingenuity is shown in averting the Rationalistic criticism of such thorny dogmas as the Trinity and the Eucharist; it is claimed that the accusation of absurdity is disproved, and therefore reason may confidently take them on authority. And again, when it is said that there is a living infallible *magisterium* in the Church, that must be accepted in a very narrow sense. The vast majority of bulls, decrees, encyclicals, &c., have only a disciplinary effect: it is piously believed by many that Providence takes a minor interest in them, but most priests take little notice of them, and the doctrine of infallibility has been carefully drawn up *not* to include them. The great dogma simply amounts to this, that the Pope (or the Church) can teach no new doctrine, but he has special guidance in his solemn declarations (which are few and far between) that certain doctrines are contained in the deposit of revelation. There have only been two such definitions in this century: Leo XIII. has not given any. Hence it will be understood how great an error those Protestants make who go over to Rome for the sake of its infallible voice (as if they were to have an infallible 'Times' at breakfast every morning), and also how untrue it is that Rome is the antithesis, the professed opponent, of reason, and only preaches submission.

No, the Church of Rome does not profess to be the refuge of the timid and the sentimental in a subversive

T

age: whatever peculiar strength it may have must be sought in its characteristic methods and institutions, not in a clear antithetic position which would make it the centre of all forces opposed to Rationalism. Those methods and institutions have been noticed in the course of the preceding narrative. In the first place, it has an organisation which is eminently superior to that of any other Christian sect, or of any religion whatever. Its constitution embodies all the several advantages of an elective monarchy and an oligarchy, indeed, it is a moot question amongst canonists whether it is to be called monarchic or oligarchic; and at the same time it avoids the instability of democratic action by theoretically dissevering its power from civil power and appealing to a higher source. Its hierarchy lends a rigid unity to its 200,000,000 of abject adherents, of which the keystone is a figure on whom a vague supernatural halo is cast, and who is now always a commanding and venerable personage. Rome, the heir of the tact, ambition, and vigour of the Cæsars, the richest treasury of art, and a veritable hive of lawyers and diplomatists, controls and utilises the talent, the ambition, and the jealousy of its great sacerdotal army, and with easy confidence commands the attention of the civilised world.

Then the completeness, the unity, and the plausibility of its theological system must be considered. From the days of St. John Damascene until the sixteenth century almost all the talent of the civilised world has contributed to the formation of that system; it is a truism to say that it is plausible. Enduring almost unchanged through ten centuries, and eliciting the veneration of almost the entire intellectual world, it presents a majestic contrast to the theologies of more recent growth. Moreover, even in recent times it has been accepted by many great writers who have left the impress of their genius upon it, and accommodated it to minds of every cast.

And side by side with the elaboration of its own system must be classed an instrument which it uses very adroitly for the same purpose, the Index Expurgatorius, or list of condemned books. In England there is little explicit mention of the Index, for economical reasons, but every Catholic is given very clearly to understand the depravity of reading books 'against faith or morals'; the restriction is cleverly represented to be a moral, not a disciplinary prescription, and thus the end of the Index is practically achieved without mentioning the odious word. Non-Catholics are gravely reminded that it is ethically imperative to study both sides of every religious question. Catholics are told in the same breath that it is sinful for them to read the works of opponents, because, naturally, they are already in possession of the truth and must not endanger its possession.

At the same time Catholics are indulged to some extent in their wayward anxiety to know what opponents are saying by having the objections formulated for them in their own apologetical literature—with satisfactory solutions appended. Here again the peculiarity of the Catholic controversial method tells in its immediate favour. As one would expect, most of the objections which are formulated have been carefully prepared for the express purpose of refutation; no Catholic writer ever gives an accurate version of hostile criticism. Newman is usually said to be the most satisfactory in this respect; in fact, it is claimed that he formulates the opinion of an adversary more lucidly than the adversary himself. But take for instance the exposition of Gibbon's five causes of the spread of Christianity in the appendix to the 'Grammar of Assent,' and compare it with the classical chapter of Gibbon; it is utterly inaccurate and unworthy. And not only are critics' opinions garbled and mutilated, but their personal characters are equally perverted. Anglicans are allowed some hope of ultimate salvation, although even here there is grave anxiety; Archbishops of Canterbury, &c., are, of course, case-hardened, men like Gladstone are fully expected to make a death-bed repentance, and so on. But when we come to greater sceptics the credit of *bona fides* is stopped: they are one and all represented to be in bad faith. Thus every Catholic believes that the Emperor Julian (the atheist, they are pleased to call him) died in a fit of rage, crying 'Galilæus vicit'; that Voltaire died raving for a priest to confess; that Döllinger and Lamennais were pride incarnate; that G. Eliot, Huxley, Tyndall, Mill, &c. &c., were beyond all plea of invincible ignorance. If a modern 'Inferno' were written it would describe a brilliant literary circle.

So also the results of philosophical, historical, and scientific research are accommodated to pious purposes. For several years geology and palæontology suffered great torture at the hands of Genesiac interpreters; history and archæology and philology then achieved marvellously convenient results; ethnology was racked to support a Biblical chronology, now abandoned; even chemistry, embryology, psycho-physics, and a host of innocent sciences were pressed into service and pressed out of shape in the process.

Of another institution which the Church formerly used for the same high purpose of guarding its flock against intellectual wolves—the Inquisition—little need be said. If it were truly a dead and discarded proceeding, like persecution on the Protestant side, it would not merit notice; it seems unprofitable to continually reproach the Church of Rome with its many and dark sins of the past of which it has really repented. However, it is not at all clear that the Church has repented of this particular outrage upon morals and humanity. The principles on which the Inquisition was founded are still part of the Church's teaching; and if it were possible to conceive a return of the ecclesiastical supremacy of former days, there is little doubt that the same policy would be urged.

Happily for many of us, civil governments are becoming more and more disinclined to be guided by ecclesiastical principles and wishes in the discharge of their function to the community. Such logical and undiplomatic writers as Dr. Ward frankly admit the inference; it is said that he found Dr. Huxley once examining his premises, and was asked by him, 'where he kept his stake for heretics?'

A second great source of strength to the Roman Church is its impressive use of æsthetic influence. The subject has been treated already, and is too conspicuous to need development. Every sense is appealed to and finds gratification in a Roman ceremony; every art is pressed into its service. In Protestant countries, where the ancient reaction against Roman corruption has reduced ceremonies to a state of spiritual nudity, this influence is found to be most potent. Indeed, a comparison of the percentage of 'converts' in different parishes with the sensuous attractiveness of their services would yield interesting results.

Other forces which are peculiarly at work in the Church of Rome can only be briefly mentioned. Its vast and powerful diplomatic body of legates, &c., and its incessant political intrigue have no parallel in any other religion; neither has the vast wealth which is contributed annually by an organised collection throughout the entire world. Owing to its profound antiquity and its comprehensive range it can enumerate a long series of humanitarian works which have been achieved by men who happened to be ecclesiastics; these become an imposing record of the Church's wondrous benefits to humanity in art, science, sociology, and philanthropy. So even in ethics the Church of Rome professes a more effective promotion of the welfare of humanity than other Churches, though in this department its claim of special power does not seem difficult to impugn.

Such would seem to be the peculiar strength of the Church of Rome in the religious struggle, as distinguished from all other Christian sects. The influences at work for its extension and consolidation are undoubtedly effective, but side by side with them it has many characteristic weaknesses which seem to give less security to its fabled immortality. In the first place, seeing that it does not shrink from and repudiate the rational criterion which the new-born age is applying to every existing institution, its very vastness is a source of danger; it presents a broader front to the keen rationalistic attack. If the mysterious dogmas which are common to all Christian sects invite criticism, nothing is gained in point of security by adding to them that microcosm of miracles— Transubstantiation— or the seven sacraments, or the vaguely floating tradition of an Immaculate Conception. Then, too, the Church of Rome is so dogmatic in its teaching, and has so frequently to abandon very positive positions. In other sects the privilege of private judgment and the absence of any adequate *magisterium* gives greater elasticity before hostile pressure.

Again the ideal of a higher life which the Church of Rome advocates brings it into collision with all modern ways of thinking. Self-torment will never again be recognised by the world at large as the supreme virtue, yet the 'saints' of the Roman calendar are honoured principally for that practice. One of the most recent models whom the Church has raised up for the veneration of humanity, Benedict Joseph Labre, shows the exemplary record of having avoided labour and lived by mendicancy, and having deliberately cultivated the most filthy habits of life. Usefulness to humanity is the principle virtue in the eyes of the modern world, and the Church pays little heed to that in canonisation. In fact, the very essence of its ethical teaching is entirely at variance with modern views; it teaches conformity with an external standard (about which there are innumerable controversies), and this for the sake of conciliating a Supreme Being and escaping His presumed vindictiveness. There is a growing tendency to regard actions which spring from such motives as non-ethical.

So, also, its insistence upon the possibility of vicarious atonement and merit is a vulnerable point; every Christian sect must, of course, admit it, but no others carry the doctrine to such length as is done in the Church of Rome. Its sacerdotal system, like that of the Jewish religion, is largely dependent on that idea; and the modern mind is diverging more and more from that attitude.

In fine, the very methods from which its strength is now derived will one day prove grievous sources of offence; for the simple reason that they are inconsistent with its real function as a purely religious organism. Diplomatic intrigue and the exercise of a purely temporal power may serve to extend and strengthen its influence in less spiritual quarters; but it is an agency of very questionable character in the hands of a spiritual body, and has more than once been the basis of an effective protest against Rome. The sensuous character of its services—a result, not of Christ's direction, but of later Roman policy—is another force of equivocal value. Any earnest thinker would scorn to be influenced by such a consideration, either as regards entering or remaining in the Church of Rome; there seems to be, even in the Church itself, a growing tendency to demand a greater purity of the religious duty. And, finally, it need hardly be said that its literary exclusiveness, its Index, its tyranny, its wilful calumniation of the character of great opponents and distortion of their criticisms, are a very vulnerable part of its system. As yet they are effective methods of preserving the integrity of the Church; but laymen are now taking the polemical work on their own shoulders, and interpreting the strictures of theologians at their own discretion—the result will be an impatient rejection of the literary restrictions which have so long insulted their intelligence and moral courage.

Such, then, are the strength and the weakness respectively of the Church of Rome in the present stage of its conflict. During its protracted existence it has encountered and triumphed over many kinds of opposition. It emerged brilliantly victorious from its secular struggle with polytheistic Rome and then with the destructive neo-Hellenism of Alexandria; it met confidently and rose upon the flood of barbarism that poured out over Southern Europe; it guided its fortunes safely through the age of iron that followed, and then controlled the fierce intellectual activity of the twelfth and thirteenth centuries; it subdued and repressed the Renaissance and almost compensated its losses in the great Reformation. But the Church has never had so varied and so powerful a host of adversaries to encounter as it has at the present day. Apart altogether from the rival Christian sects—and in point of fact these seem more disposed to friendly alliance with it than to a continued conflict—the number of opposing forces of every character, intellectual, ethical, political, and æsthetical, is a matter of grave consideration.

In the first place there is Rationalism—taking the term in its broad sense so as to include not only 'naturalism,' but also that attenuated theism which rejects orthodox Christianity in virtue of the results of the Higher Criticism. In that sense the term, of course, does not designate a single and homogeneous system, but a vast collection of distinct and militant bodies: materialism, agnosticism, positivism, pantheism, secularism, theism, and unitarianism—for these cannot be called Christian in any clear sense of the word which would not include, for instance, John Stuart Mill or Renan. They may be all safely grouped under the banner of anti-sacerdotalism, and described as a vast modern intellectual movement directed against orthodox Christianity in general and particularly against the Church of Rome, the most dogmatic, conservative, and unyielding section of Christianity and the most powerful and most skilfully organised priesthood the world has ever seen. Non-Catholic sects have no stereotyped profession, they yield and adapt themselves to pressure with curious elasticity, as is so well illustrated in 'The New Republic' of Mr. Mallock; the revolutionary movement finds its chief antagonist in the Church of Rome, which wages with it a *guerre à outrance*. How extensive that movement is, embracing all who accept the results of philosophical, scientific, and Biblical criticism, and how powerfully represented in every branch of literature, even (and conspicuously) in fiction, is too well known and too frequently pointed out by sacerdotalists themselves to be commented upon.

Then there is a distinctively modern force of an ethical character which militates against the authority of the Church. In the United States, England, and Germany, especially, a number of ethical societies have been founded and propagated with much zeal. Frequently they do not profess hostility to ecclesiastical institutions, but the mere fact that they advocate the transference of ethical life to a non-theological basis marks them out as enemies. The Church of Rome, in particular, regards herself as the only effective guardian of morality, and the ethical function of its priests is their most prominent service. It will never submit to the transfer of ethical interests to a secular institution; otherwise it would be reduced to the condition of the Greek or Roman priesthood—a condition which would not last long in modern times. Yet the ethical societies are rapidly growing in importance.

In the political world the Church has met with harsh treatment from time immemorial, and its own diplomatic power has grown keen in the long contest. But the political anti-clerical movement of modern times is in a very different position from the violent movements of that character which are dispersed throughout history. Until the last century the anti-clerical politician or diplomatist had no great anti-theological system to fall back upon. Now, the large body who are ever ready to spring up in reaction to the Church's political encroachments have a powerful philosophy to appeal to. Formerly the Church's troubles generally came from a few semi-sceptical individuals; now they spring from large political bodies, such as the Liberals of Spain and Belgium, the Libres-Penseurs of France, and the Freemasons of Italy. To the same great force must be added (from the present point of view) a new and anxiously regarded power—Socialism. The Church is very sensible of approaching danger from this quarter, and therefore, instead of its traditional practice of fierce opposition to every new movement, we find it attempting a compromise by patronising ' Christian Socialism.' This sociological force is not in direct intellectual opposition, and does not spend much time in discussing the Church's credentials; the thinkers of the modern world, it says, are fairly divided about the religious problem, and that problem has assumed most portentous dimensions—hence we busy people must be content with a mild scepticism, and if the Church crosses our path in reforming this world, so much the worse for it.

A fourth influence of a less tangible and definable character, but infinitely more dangerous in tendency and more rapid in growth, may be set down under the name of Erotism. It may be thought that this is no new danger, but the world-old revolt of human nature against that moral law whose enforcement was boldly undertaken by Christianity. But there are two considerations which make that influence, old as it is, present rather a new aspect. The first is the decay of superstition and the enfeeblement of popular faith in the supernatural. The fourteenth, fifteenth, and eighteenth centuries are marked by great outbreaks of that influence, or by the spread of public immorality; but a keen faith still lurked in the popular mind, and the Church could successfully appeal to it. A Savonarola could meet and stem a veritable tide of Hellenism. In the present division of the world of thought and the imposing opposition to ecclesiastical teaching, that simple faith must be, and is, deeply affected; and erotism gains proportionately in power and stability. The second consideration is that this erotism, or revolt against traditional ethics, has become speculative and ratiocinative, and seeks to organise its votaries and systematise its protest. The *decadence* is, perhaps, midway between practical and organised immorality; however, it is a great literary power, very widespread in France, and on the increase in England and Germany. The free-love movement has also assumed important proportions, and counts some eminent literary exponents. Most important of all, there is an æsthetic and Hellenistic school which will prove a serious adversary of traditional ethics. In practice, by a kind of *economia*, it adheres to a severe Puritanism; in theory it is revolutionary. It cherishes the higher Greek ideal of love (as found in Plato); venerates the writings of Whitman, Nietzche, and Carpenter; has all the fervour of youth and the fanaticism of ascetics.

Such are the forces which the Church of Rome, as the most prominent of the Christian churches, finds opposed to it at the threshold of the twentieth century. What the issue of the struggle will be it were presumptuous to explore; it is even a delicate task to estimate the actual condition of the Church of Rome. We have spoken in detail of the state of Catholicism in London: there it is certainly not making progress. We have had a glimpse also of its condition in the provinces, which was equally dispiriting; the immense tract of territory represented by the diocese of Northampton only contains enough Catholics to form one good congregation. Other parts of England give similar results. Take the Fylde—a long strip of the Lancashire coast—which curiously retained the old faith until modern times; I was informed by a priest who has been stationed in it for many years, at Blackpool, that Catholicism is actually decaying in the old families. On the whole, Catholicism in England seems to be stationary for the last twenty years, and promises to remain so for many years to come.

Of Catholicism abroad we can form an opinion from the religious condition of Belgium, described in the seventh chapter. The religious condition of France is well known to be highly unsatisfactory. Tested by the safe criterion of fidelity to grave obligations—such as weekly attendance at Mass and annual confession—French people seem to be fast losing their traditional faith. It is usually said, and observation of French churches seems to confirm the statement, that French women remain faithful. There is another test of fidelity which raises a serious doubt on that point. The Church of Rome is known by all its votaries to condemn neo-Malthusian practices under pain of mortal sin; they are universally and habitually employed by French women. The unusual state of its population, and the curious fact that there are in France only some 200,000 women with more than six children, throws much light on the Catholicism of France. In Germany, Rome is making progress; so also in the United States, to some extent. In Spain and Italy its influence is a mere ghost of its former power; Socialism, Liberalism, and Freemasonry, careless scepticism and erotic licence, as in France, are daily enfeebling it.

In former ages it compensated home losses by missionary conquests; its actual paltry missionary profits are little more than financial transactions. I have spoken with missionaries from every one of the great fields, and they all confirm the opinion. On public platforms, of course, they deliver set speeches, at the end of which a collection is made; but in the genial atmosphere of the sitting-room afterwards they unbend, and unequivocally represent 'conversions' of natives as money matters.

The future we leave to more acute observers and more experienced speculators. The Church of Rome, after nineteen centuries of proud unquestioned dominion, comes to the tribunal of a keenly critical, ratiocinative, utilitarian generation. In an age of universal disillusion, its venerable antiquity gives no immunity from criticism; tradition has blundered almost in every portion of its theory of human life, its religious belief must be carefully tested. The vague and shadowy forms of religion which are now so widely accepted, and which do but embody the fundamental religious instinct and tradition in one meagre and purely speculative formula, will be confident enough of acquiescence. But the Church of Rome bears the luxuriant overgrowth in dogma, and ethics, and ritual, and polity, and discipline of 2,000 years of freedom; it practically denies the activity of a purely human element in its growth, and attributes its whole intricate scheme to a divinely-guided unfolding of a divine revelation, in the face of Buddhism and other analogous growths. It appeals, too, with logic and history, not with fire and sword, or sentiment, or practical utility. And the great human consciousness that lives on and treasures up the scattered leaves of experience under the ebb and flow of endless generations, and that has at length awakened to the fact that many beliefs have been lightly imposed upon and accepted by it, will continue the struggle of its systematised thoughts through ages yet to come. But one result is even now detaching itself from the solemn struggle; a feeling of tolerance, a diminution of selfishness, a mutual trust and sympathy, a recognition that all are earnestly interpreting to the best of their power that shadow of a higher world that has somehow been cast upon the life of man.

www.ingramcontent.com/pod-product-compliance
Lightning Source LLC
Chambersburg PA
CBHW031337230426
43670CB00006B/358